Dedication

—⟋⟍—

This book is dedicated to my children, Barry Junior, Tosha, Joseph, and Jonathan. You are each a precious gift from God. Whatever you do in life, seek the Lord with all of your heart. By His Word all creation was formed. Trust in His Word will keep you close to Him. Near to Him is where you will attain the full measure of life's potential and promise. With Christ leading you, you will always find your way as the proper choices in life become clear.

"Your word is a lamp to my feet And a light to my path."
(Psa 119:105 NKJV)

Honorable Mention

—w—

The author would like to express his most sincere grati-
tude to the following people; without whose love, dedi-
cation, contribution, and faithfulness this book would not
have been possible:

Cozzette Jenkins
Paula Jenkins (Mom)
Honorable Mayor Bishop Henry W. Hearns
Dr. Jack W. Hayford
Dr. Paul G. Chappell
Reverend Bill Shumate
Dr. Mark Chironna
Ardell Rowl
Larry Cook
Reverend Bernard and Rubi Taylor
Reverend Dr. Bonnie Miller

"Render therefore to all their due: taxes to whom taxes are due, customs
to whom customs, fear to whom fear, honor to whom honor." (Rom 13:7
NKJV)

Forward

—〰—

The ultimate decision to say "YES" to the call of God lies in the hands of the one to whom the invitation is given. The Scriptural record makes it quite clear that those whom God called more often than not had a difficult time embracing the call, and afterwards a challenging time obeying the call. Part of the process of the fashioning of a servant for the sole purpose of fulfilling a place in filling up that which is lacking in the afflictions of Christ in the earth, requires the humbling and testing that the patriarchs, prophets, and apostles of old all endured. Many are indeed called, few are actually chosen.

Those who are chosen are ultimately sent with the blessing of heaven, because while no one was looking, they were being processed by the hand of God during hidden years, when others were simply enjoying their normal lives with few or little interruptions. The fiery ordeals and tests that are peculiar to one called to be a voice in their generation and a servant of the gospel are essential to being entrusted with spiritual riches. It is all too often, that in our day and age, far too many are seeking for the glitz and the glamour, seek the polish that creates a good impression, and referring to themselves as chosen by God. However, it is those who have no need to advertise themselves, have no hidden agendas, have been through the road of fiery trials, both when no one was looking and now while everyone watches, who gladly bear the burden of the Lord and walk in humility of mind as to wear the servant's towel to wash the feet of others.

Barry Jenkins invites you to a moment of truth as he openly discloses with honesty and transparency his own journey and challenge as he embraced the age-old process that Abraham, Moses, Jacob, Jeremiah, Isaiah, Peter, Paul, and countless others in Scripture went through to surrender to the highest calling and privilege known on the planet: the call to be a servant of the Lord. May this book both inspire you and clarify for you the importance of obedience and faith, and the blessing that awaits those who are called to such a high and noble calling.

Dr. Mark J. Chironna
The Master's Touch International Church

Forward

—ᴍᴍ—

Let me start by saying this is a wonderful book that is a true life story of a young man who has been there and done that, and has been left by God to live and tell about it that others may find their way and get on the road to glory. This book was written by a man who is a godly man, a true man, and a technical man.

I have personally known Barry and his wife Cozzette since 1990, and can bear witness to many of the experiences that he has shared with you.

I read the book several times and each time I found something for myself that I missed before. This short book with nineteen chapters really covers the contingencies of life that we are likely to experience throughout our lives. For instance, one subject matter deals with discouragement and promises. He shares with us the feeling of having money and yet being empty because of not having a baby. He expresses his concerns about whether or not he had the Lord's favor. His words are that God can and will use anyone. Another subject matter discusses releasing old ways.

Barry communicates about his illness and how people assumed he did not want visits while he was ill. These experiences helped him to learn that this supposition was far from the truth. However, he releases these old ideas and learns how using God's guidance just at the right time by visiting a specific person could be exactly what they needed to get them on the road to a real healing and the road to glory. In closing, this book is full of help for life's journey.

Honorable Mayor Bishop Henry W. Hearns
Senior Pastor of Living Stone Cathedral of Worship
Mayor of Lancaster, California

Introduction

—ɯʊ—

For some, a Christian walk is mapped out early in their youth. For some, the earliest hopes of a career are centered on ministry service. These are those who are groomed for God's work early on in life. They recognize the call of God and prepare a career path for the vision that God has given them.

But what about those who did not come into the knowledge of Christ until later on in life? What about those whose lives have been transformed by the Living Word? What happens when life is going by and you find yourself caught in the Master's net? When you've prepared your entire life to do things your way and your heart begins to assure you that God's way is better, how do you change course? And if He then calls you into ministry service, how do you change careers?

I would like to invite you to join me on a journey through my own experience, as the life of one man from an unlikely place discovers and embraces destiny in the service of Christ.

Pastor Barry Jenkins

Table of Contents

—ɯ—

1. In the Beginning

—m—

To begin with, this chapter is not intended to be a take on the opening words from the Bible. But, we have to start somewhere. There is no better place for me to start, other than with the road I was on when the Lord's call became clear.

The streets of New York underwent major transition during the sixties. Though much change during the early part of this decade affected the landscape, by the decade's end the change in the social atmosphere was most noticeable. This was even truer in the neighborhood we grew up in—The South Bronx.

Work was still being completed on the upper floors of this sixteen-story project building as we moved in. For the most part, the neighborhood was friendly, but that was soon to change. By the late sixties that little densely populated neighborhood we called home received its infamous nickname-Fort Apache.

Needless to say, life was tough. There were not many churchgoers in the McKinley Projects. In fact, during my entire childhood, I only knew one friend who actually went to church. The rest of the kids in the neighborhood often picked on him because he went to church.

As for us, we were not "religious." There were only two occasions on which we attended church as children. One was weddings, and the other was funerals.

Sister, Brother and myself all went to Public School 94 in the north end of the borough. From there we were all slated to go to Junior High School 80 on Moshulu Parkway. JHS 80 had, at that time, an excellent Drama Department. Each year their Drama Department would rent the City College Campus Theater, formerly known as the Bronx Community College Theater, for a two-week run of the school's drama production. During this drama production run, Elementary, High, and Junior High schools from all around the City sent busloads of students for field trips to see these plays. They were usually very good.

In our Senior year, on just such a bus trip from our Elementary School, we went to see JHS 80's production of Godspell. This was an adaptation of the Broadway musical of the same name, which depicts the Gospel in a modern setting.

The ride on the school bus to the City College Campus that year was no different than any other year. We played and had about as much fun as any sixth-graders on a field trip.

What happened during the play is something I didn't understand. All I knew was that for some reason that play touched me. In fact, so much so, that on the bus ride back to P.S. 94, one of my teachers noticed something. "What's wrong Barry?" she asked. "I don't know," I honestly replied.

It was just another play, a musical, yet there was something about this play that brought my thoughts into captivity. There was something about this play, something so very real, and yet it seemed so magical. In the mind of this sixth-grader, it must have been the magic of theater. After all, what else could it be?

From that day I was determined not only to go to JHS 80, but to be part of the Drama Department when I got there.

The next year I did go to JHS 80. Tryouts for the Drama Department began almost as soon as the semester started. There I was, more nervous than I had ever been until that time. The actual audition was short. You could hear the nervousness in my voice as I sang "I'm Stoned in Love With You" by the Stylistics.

What happened next was one of those watershed moments, where expectations and dreams converge on the road of reality. "No thank you – Not this year," Mr. Cameron said. To say I was crushed is an understatement. Since the day we saw JHS 80's drama production of Godspell, I just had to be part of something so "special."

There was no shortage of talent at JHS 80. I was not the only one who came there with high-hopes. Without a doubt I was out-gunned in the vocal department. But they were still going to need musicians to form an ensemble for that year's musical. That ensemble was going to need a drummer. And so I went home every day and practiced for hours.

That year I played percussion instruments for JHS 80's rendition of "Pippin." It was the highlight of my year, a dream come true. I was part of the magic. And for me it truly was magical. Every minute of it was a splendor, from the long hours of rehearsals, to the excitement of live performance.

Soon the production was over and the magic faded. And though these productions truly felt magical, the magic never lasted. What soared on one end to elation, fell sharply at the realization that whatever magic there was, it was only temporary.

Performing eventually became an addiction. I couldn't imagine life without playing the drums on some stage or in some nightclub. Yet somehow, it was all different than I imagined. There were no scenes in the productions I was a part of that "captured" me the way I felt the year I came to see Godspell. No applause or ovation could bring fulfillment. Something was missing. I felt empty, at the same time I felt that I needed more.

2. Watershed Moments

*I had done all that I could do. There was
something greater than me directing my
career path now.*

—ⱳ—

B y the Senior year at JHS 80, budget cuts had all but
wiped out the Drama Department. Mr. Cameron was
laid off, the JHS 80 drama legacy was over, and unbeknownst
to me, a watershed moment was near.

Many, in fact most of the students in JHS 80's Drama
and Music program, went on to either the High School of
the Performing Arts, or Music and Art. These were the two
top schools for theatrical and performing arts careers. If you
wanted a career in the performing arts field in New York, by
High School you had to be in either of these two schools.
From there, theatrical careers could go on to finish at the
world-renowned Julliard School. Being part of JHS 80's
Music Department certainly was considered a "leg up" on
such a career path.

The movie "Fame," later released in 1980, depicts one of
these two High Schools. Just to get in to the school, you had
to pass an audition. My parents felt that music lessons would
help to prepare me for these auditions. And so, I began my

"official" music studies at the renowned "Bronx House of Music."

Mr. Smith kept me on as his student even after he resigned from Bronx House. Several years were spent in study with Mr. Smith in preparation for the Music and Art School auditions. As time drew near, my sight-reading was pretty good, and Mr. Smith expressed to me that I had even surpassed him as a drummer. Yet he felt that if I went into the audition displaying "too much talent," the school would consider me unteachable. So, at his suggestion, I prepared a single snare-drum solo for my audition piece.

The piece was played flawlessly, though the interviewers seemed quite un-impressed. "Is there anything else you want to do for us?" they asked. I was petrified, while at the same time confident that Mr. Smith had prepared me well. As the interviewers posed the question I glanced over at the full "trap" set to my right. It took all the restraint I could muster up to remain focused on Mr. Smith's coaching. After all, if I really showed them what I could do, I would be un-teachable!

"No." I answered. The next several weeks went by incredibly slowly as students waited for the audition results.

Mother attended Music and Art for their Art program when she was High School age. Sister was graduating this year – also for Art. While visiting the school on Parent Teacher Night for Sister, Mother noticed the graffiti on the walls. From its social climate, the school appeared to have run down since mother's attendance.

After a few visits to her old Alma Mater, mother wasn't too excited at the thought of me going to Music and Art. She knew I also had interests in aerospace, and encouraged me to test at Aviation High School in Long Island City, Queens.

In contrast, Aviation was ranked among the top academic High Schools in New York City. In all honesty, it was a bit too neat and clean for my taste at that time. Nevertheless I took the entrance examinations for Aviation High School at mother's urging (as if I had a choice).

Barry Wasserman was my Band Teacher at JHS 80. He often expressed that I was perhaps the most promising student he ever had. Mr. Wasserman often asked me to tutor prospective drummers during the lunch hour.

When the news came that Music and Art did not accept me, I was crushed. It was surreal. Even Mr. Wasserman could not believe that his "most promising student" had not been accepted.

Ironically, the school that I was least interested in getting into, the school with some of the highest scholastic requirements in all of New York – they wanted me. Here I was, being given an opportunity of a lifetime, and it really didn't mean anything to me. It wasn't what I wanted. It wasn't my first choice.

In spite of all the training, in spite of all my hard work, in spite of the fact that I was already a working drummer with recording deals, the "door was slammed shut" on any aspirations I had for the performing arts. Just getting through Aviation meant there was not going to be time for gigs or musical engagements.

All that effort, and I was still powerless to choose my own destiny. I had at that time a sense that I was being led on a road that was not of my own choosing. For me, choices became limited. I had done all that I could do. There was something greater than me directing my career path now. But not just my career, my future, and my life.

3. Engineering 101

It was the job of a lifetime. Yet with all that this job was, with all that it made me feel, I was still empty.

—⁓—

I did go to Aviation High School. It was, at first, a difficult time for me, a time of adjustment from what seemed like shattered dreams. Music was more than a fantasy – it represented my "ticket" out of the South Bronx, out of the trauma of life in Fort Apache, out of a difficult home life. Nevertheless, all heartaches, fears, and phobias were ultimately conquered, as I went on to graduate among the top ten percent of my class.

The "brass ring" for any graduate from Aviation High School was a license from the Federal Aviation Administration. It was a license that permitted its bearer to work on aircraft. If obtained, it meant that its holder was immediately employable anywhere in the aerospace field.

Obtaining an FAA license at Aviation High School meant putting in the overtime. It's a notable accomplishment for any high school student. So much so, that upon graduation the license holder actually received two high school diplomas – one is a customary academic diploma, and the other an FAA diploma.

The average school day was twice that of other high schools. In addition to standard high school academia, there were long hours each day that had to be spent in hangar and shop facilities gaining the knowledge and experience requirements which were prerequisite just to take the FAA licensing exams.

By God's grace I made it through all of the prerequisites and passed all of the written, practical, and oral FAA exams. So here I was, eighteen years old, and licensed to work on aircraft. What tremendous opportunity at such a young age! "Winds of change" were rising up through the annuls of my life.

It was a wonderful time in life. I was young and, in my mind, at the "top of my game." Dad knew I needed a car, so he called a co-worker at a Midas Muffler shop in Yonkers where he once worked. "We still have a deal?" Dad asked. After getting off the phone Dad threw a rope and a six-pack of beer in the trunk of his car.

When we got to that Midas shop, Dad gave his friend twenty-five dollars and the six-pack of beer he brought in the trunk. Then Dad tied one end of the rope around the bumper of his car, and the other end of the rope onto this blue car. It was a '65 Ford Mustang that had severe body rot and was missing one of the front seats. From the inside rear seat, you could see the ground through the rotting floor panels.

Dad used his car to tow while I steered the Mustang. It wasn't much to look at, but it was a Mustang, and it was going to be mine. When we got home he helped me to push the car into our back-yard. As he threw me the keys, Dad said, "You want it, you fix it."

That summer I got to put into practice many of the skills acquired at Aviation High School. Dad and I built a make-shift engine hoist and pulled the frozen engine out of the car.

In the hot summer months that engine was dismantled in the smallest detail and rebuilt right there in our back yard.

Things seemed to be falling in place. While rebuilding the Mustang, I accepted a job offer to go work for a small aircraft maintenance company in Ashland, Virginia. By summer's end, the Mustang project was finishing up just as the start date approached for this, my first job in aircraft. The schedule couldn't have been cut any closer. Just as the car started for the first time, I threw my luggage in the back and headed off to the new job.

Looking back it's evident the Lord was with me. Here I was, about to start a new life, embarking on a four-hour drive, in the pouring rain, in a fifteen-year-old automobile with an untested engine. But, by the Lord's grace, the journey was without incident, and I made it in time to start the new job.

It was exciting and unnerving all at the same time. There were many firsts for me during that season—my first car, my first apartment, my first real job, and my first real-life-lesson in "culture shock."

Work itself at that little hangar in Ashland, Virginia was rewarding. It took some getting used to the social climate though.

As we worked on the aircraft, the boss would often tell "Black" jokes while the crew laughed and encouraged him on—that is, everyone but me.

About two months into the job I asked Dad if he would help me out by bringing down a 1/4" ratchet set from New York. I was young and naïve. I wanted dad to see me on the new job, I wanted my boss to meet the man who inspired me, my hero, my father.

My boss Steve and I stood there outside of the hangar as my parents drove near and parked. From our vantage point we really couldn't see who was in Dad's Chevy van.

He came out of the car and walked about a hundred-fifty feet to where Steve and I were standing. "Is that your dad?"

"Yes, I said. As Dad approached Steve, he reached out to shake Steve's hand. As their hands embraced Steve said, "Good evening Mr. Jenkins, I think busing is a good thing. . ."

It was one of those awkward moments in the wake of which you knew that life was about to change somehow. It was a bump, a jolt, felt as life appeared to be going very smoothly. All of my recent hopes, dreams, and expectations seemed to be riding on success at this, my first job in the career that took so much to launch. Little did I know that my road was about to take a major detour.

I was embarrassed at the blatant racial overtone that Steve brought to bear upon meeting my father. It was more than I could imagine or take. And I expected it was more than my dad was going to take. At any moment I thought my dad was going to "lose it" and give this man a knuckle sandwich.

Yet, Dad handled the situation with the utmost poise and grace. He did not show even the appearance of offence, as they talked on for about fifteen minutes. Then the door of the van opened and Mom came walking towards us. Steve looked at her, saw only that she was white, and said to my father, "Who's that, the maid?" "That's my wife," Dad said. With that, Steve uttered a few words in the "French vernacular" and promptly stormed off.

From that day, Steve would not allow me to work on any of the aircraft. From that day the only job he would allow me to do was to sweep the floors. By week's end Steve called me into the office and informed me that I was being laid off.

After that brief assignment in Virginia, I packed up everything in the Mustang, drove back home to New York City, and went immediately to the Employment Center back at Aviation High School. "So you need another job, Barry?" asked Mr. Robert Kyle, Assistant Principal. "Yes," I said. "Be here tomorrow, Lockheed will be here hiring." That very next day, after a grueling interview, Lockheed offered me a job with their "Skunk Works" division in Burbank, California.

So here I was, back at my parent's home in New York after what was a brutal lesson in culture shock. But this lesson gave me time to think, time to ponder if there was some force perhaps leading me, guiding me from the intricacies of my own vision onto a road with a much grander scheme.

Beginning this new career down in Virginia I was "gung ho," ready to give, willing to give, and, in fact, giving my all. But the door closed for me there shortly after my arrival. And while that door closed, another opened, providing a pathway for a new journey. It was a journey that would lead me far away from the comfort zone of my parents' home in New York. It was farther than this teenager had ever imagined.

Though admittedly overwhelmed at the proposition of moving three thousand miles from home, I accepted the new job with Lockheed and made flight arrangements bound for Los Angeles.

Upon leaving New York, it stormed so bad that the nose wheel of the 747 Jumbo Jet was moving several feet from side to side as the plane loaded. That scene itself should have been enough to deter me from leaving, but it didn't. There was no future for me in New York; there was nothing behind me. The only path available to me that night was to board that flight.

There was little time to think about a musical career anymore. I was nineteen, had been given a job of great responsibility for a major aircraft manufacturer. By then it was clear that stability was of paramount importance. The life of a struggling musician would be anything but stable, and by then I had a pregnant girlfriend to care for.

Of course that old Mustang was so ridden with body rot that I thought it best to leave it back at my parents' home rather than attempt to drive it cross-country. No, this new road I was on had great demands, and it required a vehicle that could be depended on. Besides, cars in Los Angeles didn't rust the way cars did on the East coast.

After arriving in Los Angeles, I quickly found another car. It was a fairly decent '69 Mustang that was white with black leather interior. Most important, you could put your feet down in the back seat without them touching the ground beneath the car.

The training at Aviation paid off. Within two years Lockheed advanced me to the rank of Junior Design Engineer – Aircraft Structures.

If there was ever a time when opportunity knocked, this was it! This job was quite literally the envy of anyone who aspired to enter the aerospace engineering field! By twenty-one, I was yet without a college degree, and had an enviable job in the "super secret" Skunk Works designing the most advanced state-of-the-art aircraft technologies ever conceived.

Just to set the record straight, by then I did have some college and some engineering training. My point is that for what little education I had, this opportunity was beyond comprehension, and still is!

If it were at all possible to derive some sense of conquest, some pride, and even a bizarre sense of glory, it was here. I was among the privileged few who ever got to see behind the "veil of secrecy." But, not only to see, to actually be one of the people who determined what that scene looked like!

To this young man at that time, it was the most fulfilling job that could be imagined. My colleagues were respected around the world for their engineering accomplishments. The Skunk Works was "world renowned" for turning out the most technologically-advanced aircraft in existence. The greatest aerospace engineering minds in the world worked to my left and to my right. They enjoyed "passing on" tidbits to "bring me up to speed."

The facility where I worked was nestled amongst the runways of the Burbank Airport, a short distance from the glamour of the Burbank Studios. Building 90 was a four-story aluminum-clad building. There was no "front entrance," but a small opening cloaked in its rear through which those entering and exiting were routinely subject to search.

After dawning identification and successfully negotiating past the guards, there was an elevator which only went as high as the third floor. From there the scene was reminiscent of the opening trailers from the old "Get Smart" television series. There were corridors and doors with cipher locks on them. Each segment required a greater level of security access. The correct door opened to another chamber, whose concealed escalator whisked you to the next level. Beyond that were more doors surrounding the Design Group. It was a large room with drawing boards everywhere, and near its center was mine.

As I reflect on those days at Bldg 90, being young and impressionable, it was as if God Himself placed me in the midst of not only the finest aeronautical engineering minds in the world, but with God-fearing individuals of the highest integrity. The combined influence of such people "seasoned" my heart, infusing it with faith and clarity in view of the true and eternal Christ, which was demonstrated by their forbearance.

Ironically this building was named "Building 90." In geometric terms, a ninety degree turn is a turn completely perpendicular to the path you are taking. It was in this building that God exposed this young man to a different life. A life where men of integrity held to different values than I was accustomed to. A life where the promise of integrity was made manifest by personal accomplishments. It was in this setting that God altered the course of my life forever.

It was the job of a lifetime. Yet with all that this job was, with all that it made me feel, in the end I was still empty.

Things in my personal life were pretty bad. My girlfriend and I married, but that marriage was short-lived and ended bitterly. We had two children, and though I retained custody of my son, I lost custody of my daughter. Both she and her mother relocated back to New York, and contact with my daughter became virtually impossible.

Separation from my daughter was, for me, a daily torment. With a certainty, the relief I imagined that divorce would afford never came. Instead, there was a constant reminder, a prevailing pain in the midst of a broken home.

In the days and months that followed the separation, work became a place to go and reflect. Reflect on my life, my failures, and my triumphs. I suppose that it was during this time that I began to understand that this highly-coveted job could never bring the fulfillment I longed for.

Lockheed felt my work worthy of promotion, and advanced me from my status as "Junior" Design Engineer to Design Engineer. I've met people whose entire lives were devoted to career paths that would get them to where I had already arrived by the age of twenty-four. This is not some self-imposed piety or pompous point of view. While working, I took engineering classes in college. Many classmates aspired to the position I held at work.

Yet, during those lonely days at work after the separation, there was one question that resounded over and over in my mind – "Why?" The job had become so mundane that I could almost do it in my sleep. The novelty had worn off, and the drudgery set in. What it all came down to was a routine of coming to work to sit in front of a computer screen or a drafting board and drawing lines all day.

The pressure was always on to "put down" more lines in a shorter amount of time with each new Skunk Works project. There was always a race against time to complete a given number of blueprints. It was no longer fun for me.

It became monotonous. And so, I began to take a good hard look at why I was doing what I was doing.

There were some obvious conclusions to questions that raced through my mind. "What else could I do?" "Who else would hire me without a college degree?" These were just some of the rationale that kept me there.

But, whenever I asked myself why I stayed at the Skunk Works, there was one overwhelming response my thoughts eluded to – "The glory."

Being a "growing babe" in Christ, having accepted Jesus as Lord and Savior several years earlier, glory was quickly becoming an unacceptable reason for staying on this job.

It was pride, plain and simple. I liked hearing the "oooohs, and the ahs" whenever I told someone what I did for a living. There was a flavor of celebrity-ism, a sense of distinct privilege of working in this high-tech development arena cloaked in secrecy.

Pride and personal glory, that's what it came down to, and I was becoming increasingly aware that it was wrong. Neither facet, either pride or glory, could bring the fulfillment I longed for.

In the wake of this difficult and thought-provoking time came one of the most meaningful discoveries of my life. Job fulfillment and life fulfillment are two different things. Often we pursue one by mortgaging or even bankrupting the other. Yet, is it possible to have them both? Is it possible to have job fulfillment *and* life fulfillment? Is it possible to find a *balance*? One thing is certain, that unless God orders your steps, your destination will not find lasting fulfillment. As we learn to put Him first, even the testimonies He gives us provide counterbalance for our journey.

4. Building Testimonies

It was almost as if God was saying in that dream, "I'm preparing you for something, and it's alright."

—⁓—

O f course as an engineer I wasn't driving that old white '69 Mustang anymore. I was moving up the "career path" now, and needed a car that could navigate the new roads of my *status*.

It was my first new car. I had my eyes on it for some time. It was a 1983 Nissan Maxima, complete with metallic blue paint, a sun roof, aluminum alloy wheels, and a five-speed manual transmission that drove like a rocket. Yet even with the car and the career, there was still emptiness, a feeling that I wasn't being fulfilled.

By this point in my life, I was convinced that if there was going to be anything permanent, anything truly fulfilling, it was going to take God to arrange it. I had failed at one marriage, and didn't want to endure that heartache ever again. And so in the order of Hezekiah's prayer, I wrote down all what I wanted in companionship, placed that list on my bed, and prayed earnestly over it.

By 1985 I met Cozzette, and seemingly overnight we became the best of friends. Of all the things on my prayer list, Cozzette by far exceeded them. Without a doubt this prayer was heard and answered. We were soon to be married.

Like any new couple, we began to plan and prepare for our future. Together we opened B&W Computer Systems in Van Nuys. Though still working for Lockheed, it was one of our dreams - to become independent. We also prayed that we could buy our own home someday soon.

With being newlyweds, having a new business, working full time, and raising Barry Jr., one thing we failed to do in those early years was to find a home church. Neither of us were mature enough in our faith to realize that God should have come first if there were to be any lasting attainment of success.

What we did instead was to promise God, that if He would answer our prayer and bring us into a home of our own, we would in turn dedicate ourselves to finding a home church. And so we ran our business and worked hard to save towards our home.

Within a few short years after we were married, Cozzette's mother was diagnosed with cancer. Neither of us had ever lost anyone close to us before. LeGurtha suffered through surgeries and ultimately succumbed to her illness. It was hard watching Cozzette grieve as her mother suffered and passed. Life for us was beginning, but it was marked with tragedy.

What happened during that time was something I can only describe as God's grace. One night while asleep, I dreamt that I was in a limousine somewhere in New York. In that limousine I clearly saw my own mother, sister, brother, and Barry Jr. all dressed up. Suddenly, the car we were in was struck from behind. The next thing I remember, we were walking down a slight hill, and passed through an archway with a sign that read "Ferncliff." Mother was crying, and I had a desire to spend time with her, yet I knew that my job at Lockheed was not going to allow me more time off.

When I awoke from that dream, I had an overwhelming sense that I needed to see my father. In fact, I was quite distraught about it and could not understand why.

Cozzette and I sent Dad a plane ticket, and he visited us for three weeks. During that time there was much healing of some childhood issues that previously hindered our relationship. We had a great time together, Dad, Cozzette, Barry Jr., and I. During his visit with us, Dad complained about some chest pains and mentioned that he needed to see his doctor when he got back to New York.

His trip concluded wonderfully. We were all overjoyed with the visit. It was a few weeks after he returned home when we got the news that my father had been diagnosed with inoperable lung cancer.

The following months involved a lot of "course correction" as preconceptions and ideals were dismantled.

If there was one thing that I could count on, it was my father's word. He never lied to me, and whatever he said, well, that's the way it was. When I spoke to him after his diagnosis, Dad told me not to worry. He said that he was "going to beat this thing." And with those words, I trusted and was not afraid.

Living and working three thousand miles away from your family makes times like this difficult, to say the least. There were close calls as the cancer began to "take its toll." The distance made being there difficult to impossible.

Back then, "Emergency Family Leave" from work was up to the manager's discretion, and my new manager, well, let's just say he wasn't very understanding.

When the cancer spread to his brain, Dad was hospitalized. He was semi-comatose and the doctors were not expecting him to survive the night. At that time, I was able to get a leave from work to fly home and be there by his side.

In his hospital room he was surrounded by medical staff; who had essentially "written him off" and were neglecting to give Dad the care he needed. After getting the staff to care for some basic things, I asked them to step outside so I could spend some time in prayer with my father.

Dad didn't pass that night or that week; in fact he recovered somewhat after that night and was able to get around a little bit. We all breathed a sigh of relief as Dad appeared to be on the road to recovery. Then, about seven months later, Dad's condition turned, and he lost his battle with cancer.

As I sat there in the limo on the way to Dad's burial, there was sense of deja-vu when instantly the limo was struck from the rear by a car transport truck. Oddly enough I was comforted, as that mysterious dream came back to my remembrance and I knew everything was going to be alright. After the burial we walked down a slight hill and I saw the arch that bore the name of the cemetery "Ferncliff."

The grieving process was painfully difficult, to say the least. Yet, there was a strange comfort. It was the comfort of knowing that God granted me those three weeks. Because of that dream, Dad and I shared a time of closeness, a time of healing, a time of friendship. It was a dream whose meaning was elusive and left me with an overwhelming desire to spend time with my father.

Did God send the dream? I believe so. Could God have healed my father? Of course. Yet, for His own reasons, He chose not to. Through it all, God, in the riches of His mercy, graced me with a final season with my dad, and He did it through a dream.

That God would do this for me was mind-boggling. I was not in a home church. In fact, in all honesty, I was not living a Christian life much at all, though I was seeking Him. At that time, the most God had from me was a confession that He is Lord, and a promise to find a home church after finding a home.

There was no question in my mind that this dream had been Divine intervention, inspiring me to spend time with Dad. The only question in my mind was, "Why?" After all, I was nobody special. In fact, there were many areas of my life that could only be described as complete failure. Whatever pristine reputation thought to represent my youth had long since tarnished.

Why would God care enough about this broken man, a man who already logged surmountable personal failures? A man who was not raised religious? A man who seldom darkened the threshold of any church? Why would God grant such a man as me those three precious weeks with my father? And why would He grant me that time through a dream?

The answer that resonates in my soul is that it was all part of God's divine purpose.

That dream had a profound impact on my life, as well as Cozzette's life. It wasn't about us, our accomplishments, or our failures. Through this experience, God moved our hearts. It was as though He saw in the hardened soil a stone. And after having picked it out of the dirt, He brushed it off and began to contemplate what He would make of it.

Likewise, this dream and this season so moved us from a place of hardened comfort. Through the events that surrounded us, through the grief we each felt in the loss of a parent, our hearts were becoming pliable in the Master's hands. Our lives were about to take shape, and once again the road we were on was about to change course.

In retrospect, it was as if God were saying in that dream, "I'm preparing you for something, and it's alright." During that season of preparation, God taught us many lessons about trust and about prayer. We began to realize that God will reveal Himself intimately through prayer.

5. Answered Prayers

When we came to Living Stone Cathedral of Worship, there was no question, that's where we were supposed to be. . .

—⚎—

God is not so far away that He can not hear the still small voice of a quiet seeker, or show Himself mighty in personal and indisputable ways. For us, we were entering a "season of revelation," where God provided the assurance of His presence and the guarantee of His comfort. In His loving-kindness, He "winked" at our inabilities and our fledgling faith, and looked beyond to the destination that could only be reached by faith.

For those who seek Him, He knows exactly how to touch them, He knows precisely how to reach a person's heart to cause his or her direction to alter, and the seeker finds eventuality at the place of God's predestination.

As for me, I made career plans like anyone else. Those plans were laboriously worked as time went on and challenges were presented. Little did I know that down the road there was another plan, a plan not of my ingenuity, but it was a plan of divine conception.

During the time of Dad's last visit with us, Cozzette and I were running our fledgling computer business from our apartment. By day I went to work at Lockheed and at night built computers.

Cozzette handled most of the "business" side of things. We bought our second "new" car, a plush 1986 Mazda B2000 Club Cab pick-up. While I was at work, she took our new pick-up and purchased the parts needed to build the computers.

"Word of mouth" was getting around, and soon we had more business than we could handle from that tiny apartment. We rented a storefront across the street from our apartment.

It was quite a challenge getting the store ready to open for the first time. We learned quickly that a commercial property is much more expensive to open and operate than an apartment. In addition to the rental fees, there were "triple net" and other fees. Today I still don't think I really understand what "triple net" fees are!

Moreover, the deposits required for turning on each utility was at least ten times what a residential utility cost. After all this, there were still licenses, permits, fees, taxes and insurance to pay for.

Once we began the process of opening the business it became a "race against time" to get the business "up and running" and to start making enough profit just to cover all of the monthly expenses.

During those days we came to an impasse. We had fixed it up about the best we could get it, the store was just about ready to open, but there was one final expense we had not considered. Because it was a computer business, the electric utility required a five-hundred-dollar security deposit before they would turn on service. This was still the late 80's, and five hundred dollars at that time was a lot of money. We were "spent out." Just about all we had was already tied up in the new store.

Spiritually speaking, we were "young in Christ." For me it was as though the fire within me that yearned for God was being smothered by the concerns of everyday life. I had Christ, but He was an "addition" to everything else in my life and had not yet become the "sustenance" of my life.

What follows is a lesson in prayer and God's provision. It's a testimony that was several years in the making.

Neither Cozzette nor I yet knew how to trust God for provision, and were not wholly convinced yet that our prayers were even being heard. Our faith was weak, and our devotional life was desolate.

Though I believed in God, my knowledge of Him was limited, and as a result I trusted more my abilities than His provision. In short, I prayed for God to provide, but had my own ideas of <u>how</u> God should answer my prayers.

And so here we were, having gone as far as we could in our own abilities. Our hopes and dreams were tied up in a store that was almost ready to open. Yet, in spite of our best efforts, that dream was five hundred dollars beyond our reach. This place of our shortfall was precisely the place God chose to orchestrate a lesson in humility, faithfulness, provision, and prayer.

One evening, as Cozzette and I sat in the new store contemplating how we could raise the five-hundred-dollars needed to turn on the electricity and "open up shop," Bernie came by.

Bernie, his wife Ruby, and I, had worked at the same facility at Lockheed for several years. At about the same time Cozzette and I were opening our business, Bernie was "on fire" for the Lord, as someone who just discovered fine gold.

He walked into the "tech room" of our store and we talked for a little while. Then came something I didn't expect or even know how to deal with. "The Lord told me to come over here today and do this," Bernie said, as he laid five-hundred-dollars on the work bench.

To me, that moment was very awkward. It was the exact amount of money I prayed for. Though that money was so desperately needed, I did not know how to accept it. After all, if it was God answering my prayer, He would do it some other way than have someone I didn't know all that well just walk right in and lay it down, wouldn't He?

In hindsight, it was a subtle mixture of pride and ignorance that won out, because that day I would not accept Bernie's gift.

And so Cozzette and I "pressed on," leveraging paychecks, cashing in savings bonds, soliciting family. Eventually we "got it together" and opened the store.

In those days it seemed as if no matter how many computers we sold we were always five-hundred-dollars behind. Even as our business grew, we seemed to stay the same five-hundred-dollars behind on our obligations.

Eventually our business grew to the point where we could no longer function in the tiny storefront. We leased a second storefront in the same complex to get the extra space needed. By this time we had several full-time employees, and our monthly "shortfall" grew from five hundred to two-thousand-dollars.

Back at the ranch; there's something about tragedy that makes you stop and think. I was still grieving over the loss of my father. Working conditions at Lockheed had degraded with changing regimes.

Regime changes are something that most of us have to live with from time to time in some form or fashion. For me, this season at Lockheed presented most difficult challenges.

There was a co-worker who worked a few feet across from me for years. Perhaps I didn't try hard enough to "get along" with him. Whatever the reason, he was vocal about the fact that he never cared for me being there. Then one day, he suddenly became my department manager, my boss.

This change in the work environment came as Cozzette grieved over the loss of her mother and I was losing my dad.

For years I went to work feeling that any career change would be "a step down" from my prestigious job at Lockheed. It was an enviable job complete with intrigue and mystery. Yet, for some reason, as I grew closer to the Lord, I began to understand that my reasons for staying there were my own sense of job-satisfaction and personal glory.

After Dad passed I began to question being there. Pride and glory were no longer strong enough to hold me, it just didn't seem worth it to stay any more, and so I left the "job of a lifetime," and Cozzette and I ran the business full-time.

About that time, we learned how difficult it is to qualify for a home loan when you are self-employed. Without a verifiable paycheck, bank lenders can only look at your taxable income records to make a loan determination. When you are in business for yourself, the tendency is to claim every entitlement and reduce your tax liability as much as allowable. So then the dilemma becomes finding a way to prove your income without sacrificing legitimate deductions.

Faced with these difficulties, Cozzette and I prayed that God would "make a way" for us to buy a home. We promised Him that if He would get us into a house, that we would find a church home and devote ourselves to Him. By the winter of 1990, God answered our prayers and we were in our new home.

For nearly a year after we moved in our house, one excuse after another kept us from finding a church home. Sure, we looked around and even visited, but nothing felt like home. We promised God that we would get into a church home after we moved into our house, and now it was time for us to live up to that promise. And so we began to pray that God would lead us to the place where He wanted us to worship.

There were many churches in the Antelope Valley to choose from. We visited many of them, but had difficulty finding one we were all comfortable with.

Somewhat frustrated at finding the right church, I began to contemplate who would know where the church was that would be a good fit for my family. As any reasonable young man would do, I turned to the main source of regional information, my barber, Pete.

Pete told me about a church in Littlerock, which was about ten miles east of my home. It was a fairly large church which was, at that time, called First Missionary Baptist Church, but later became known as the Living Stone Cathedral of Worship.

When we came to Living Stone Cathedral of Worship there was no question that's where we were supposed to be.

What a struggle! In those early days, it seemed like there was always a problem on the way to church. Either we began fussing at each other, or we woke up late. There was always something that tried to distract us from getting to church. Yet, we knew that we had to "push through" the difficulty.

We knew that our spiritual life was lacking. The effects of this void were widespread. We wanted something. We needed something. What we wanted and needed was only to be found on the other side of the church doors.

Faith was not something we just automatically had by virtue of having accepted Jesus as Savior. We knew we were lacking in this area. The first class we signed up for at Living Stone Cathedral of Worship was "How to Develop Your Faith." As our faith was fed, as we exercised faith and listened to God's Word, our faith began to grow.

Charlie Watkins was a minister at the church who "took us under his wings," so to speak. He would come over on Fridays to read through the Bible with us and encourage us.

At first, it seemed that as our faith grew, our mortgage grew further and further behind. We structured our finances to handle the business's needs first, then pay our house bills after the store's bills were paid. After all, we were now fully reliant on our business for our income.

While at our home for Bible study one evening Charlie noticed that I seemed a bit preoccupied and asked what was wrong. "On Monday morning, the bank starts foreclosure proceedings on our new house," I answered.

As Charlie began to pray for us, he got very quiet. After a few moments he turned to me and said, "The Lord said that when you started your business someone tried to give you some money, I don't know what that amount is, but whatever it was you would not accept it."

Immediately Cozzette and I felt "goose bumps." We hadn't told anybody about the time Bernie tried to help us when we were short on money to get the store open. For the record, we did not attend the same church as Bernie, who lived an hour away, nor did we have any church friends in common. In short, neither Bernie nor Charlie knew each other. There was no way for Charlie to know about that incident unless God revealed it to him.

Charlie had our attention, as there was little doubt in our minds that he was hearing from God.

We told Charlie he was right, and shared with him how Bernie tried to help us when we started out in business. Charlie confirmed that this was in fact what the Lord was showing him.

Up until that night I never really understood the principle of "giving and receiving." In my prideful arrogance, I previously felt that it was I who had to be the one giving – especially with anyone other than a close family member.

Charlie explained to us how God did, in fact, give Bernie instruction to bless us with that money two years earlier. He went on to say how our failure to accept this blessing not only hindered our immediate need, but also hindered Bernie's blessings from the Lord. In fact, by not accepting his gift, we were hindering the blessings that God had for Bernie, which were to be released by virtue of his giving to us.

This was a new concept for us. Not only is there a blessing for us as we give, but when we receive a gift we have a role in facilitating a blessing for the giver. It's not just about *our* seed and *our* harvest. It's also about allowing our brethren to sow a seed into our lives to propagate his harvest, and all increase is from God.

God used Charlie and our difficult financial situation that night to teach us a lesson. It was a lesson we would not have understood any other way. When our pride keeps us from receiving, we can "short circuit" not only our own prayers, but we inhibit prayers and blessings that God has in store for those He chooses to help us.

Confronted with this realization, we felt shame and grief. There was no more pride. In its place was the knowledge that we stood on the verge of losing the home we labored so hard to get into, and we were losing it because of pride.

Charlie got quiet. He said the Lord was speaking to him again. Then he told us, "Before you do anything else on Monday, go see that man. . . . He still has your blessing for you." Then Charlie went on to say, "And that you know that this is from God, whatever that amount was, it has multiplied by four."

Well, at this point the goose bumps faded and skepticism set in. I wanted to believe. I needed to believe. Our house was about to go into foreclosure and we needed exactly four times the amount Bernie first tried to give us. Again, Charlie had no way of knowing these details.

When Charlie left that night, I didn't know what to think. Since I didn't have the faith to trust God for the original five-hundred, how was I going to have faith to trust God for two-thousand?

The following Monday was no different than any other Monday. Neither Cozzette nor I spoke about the things that Charlie said to us. We hadn't seen Bernie in quite some time, and hadn't really kept in touch over the years.

We opened up the store and within a few minutes I received a call to go work on someone's computer system. Seeing it as a "bird in the hand" I took off immediately to take care of the service call.

Upon my return, Cozzette said, "Bernie was here looking for you." Could it be that what Charlie said to us last Friday night was real? Could it be that God cared enough about us to provide all the money we so desperately needed? One thing was for sure, I was going to find out!

When I arrived at his home and knocked on the door, Bernie answered and said, "Hello, Barry, I've been expecting you." He went on to say how three days earlier, while fasting, the Lord spoke to him. Just then he handed me an envelope and said; "Now I've been wrestling with this for years, and I'm not going to wrestle with this no more!" I took the envelope from him and put it in my shirt pocket.

Bernie invited me in and ministered to me from First and Second Kings, about how Elijah fled from Jezebel, and how Elisha remained with Elijah through many hardships.

When I returned to the store Cozzette asked, "Well, what happened?" "He gave me this envelope," I answered. Just then I took the envelope out of my pocket and opened it together with Cozzette. There it was. It was just as Charlie described. It was two-thousand-dollars, exactly four times what we refused to accept from Bernie the first time. It was exactly what we needed to keep our house from foreclosure.

The Lord revealed Himself mightily in our deliverance that day. God's timing is still remarkable to us. Not only did He provide the finances we needed, but he gave us a glimpse of His majesty in that the very moment He was speaking to us through Charlie three days earlier, it was the same time

49

that God was providing our solution by speaking to the heart of a man who was in prayer and fasting an hour's journey away. This was a divine "conference call" conducted without the aid of technology. It was a miracle whose origins were from His Majesty Himself.

Prior to this experience, I felt that "God helps those who help themselves," and truly He does. But that doesn't preclude other ways in which God helps His people. At once we received a lesson in faith, a lesson in humility, and the financial lesson which came with the blessing we so needed.

Bernie and Ruby have been angels sent to us by God. Their obedience is an example of faithfulness. From our Christian "baby steps" to baptism, this blessed couple has taken us into adoption as their own younger brother and sister.

By now we were learning to trust God. He ministered to us in ways that no one could understand. He answered all of our prayers. There was no question that God was real. The only question we had left was, "How do we learn to trust Him more?" Perhaps a better way to phrase that is, "How do we learn not to trust in ourselves?"

Our life together began almost simultaneously with our decisions to devote our lives to Christ. If I were counseling a couple seeking to get married today, what I would say is that this is the hard way to do things.

What I mean by this is that Cozzette and I were newly-weds. Settling into each other's lives, adjusting to parenting and step-parenting, building a business and moving into a new home – these are all tremendous weights to bear when first seeking God.

Is there ever an opportune time to (first) seek God? Perhaps not. However, anyone contemplating marriage would be best prepared by developing a strong relationship with Christ first.

God's idea of marriage is that one plus one equals one. In other words, one complete person in Christ joins in marriage with another complete person in Christ. The result is oneness together in Christ that in effect lends adhesive properties to the marriage. A primary relationship with God whereby the couple both understand His word and relate to His heart will give needed strength during difficult times.

Youthful exuberance can blind a couple into thinking that one broken person plus one broken person makes one well person. Not that either Cozzette or I were broken in any external or obvious way. In fact, by then we both knew God, and understood that a relationship with Jesus was essential for each of us.

Yet there were things we could have done which would have made for a "smoother transition" to life together. The most obvious would have been to make finding a home church our highest priority. Once at a church home, pre-marital classes with the pastor would have helped equip us for life together.

The point here is that there is an easy way and a hard way of doing things. Putting God first is always the easy way. Thankfully, Cozzette is a woman of great character, who sought the Lord together with me.

As a pastor, I have seen that all too often a young couple enters into a marital commitment thinking that if it doesn't work out, they can quickly get a divorce.

Our society throws around accolades like "closure" to disguise the unholy effects of divorce. But the truth is that divorce is a wicked violence, an unholy selfishness, in whose counsel there is no such thing as closure.

Sadly enough, even in the Christian community some people will attempt to use the Bible to justify their selfish decision. Yet divorce is not God's plan, but is derived from bitterness and hard-heartedness.

*"He said to them, 'Moses, because of the hardness of your hearts, permitted you to divorce your wives, but from the beginning **it was not so**.'" (Mat 19:8 NKJV)*

The best way to avoid divorce is to allow God to form you completely before getting married. As we, through Christ, discover and work out the hardened areas of our hearts, as the stony places become fallowed in His hands, then we become ready to adhere to the blueprint for living together which God has given us.

In order to make a functional product and get it to market, every manufacturing facility must have two components. First you need engineers. These are the designers, if you will, whose concepts are detailed in plans such that others can follow the plans and build the product. Then there is the "production component," whose responsibility it is to make the product according to the blueprint's dimensions.

It is the designer that "lays out" the parameters of the product. These parameters determine how far you can go in every dimension in order that the part can fulfill its intended purpose. It is the designer who gives the tolerance limitations, which say how far "off the mark" any dimension can be before the part becomes scrap.

God is the designer and the architect of marriage. We are at best that "production" component, charged with making the finished product look like the "blueprint." The dimensions (or parameters) of our lives have already been drawn out.

All of God's dimensioning for us has been drafted in His Testaments. In order for the finished product (in this case, marriage) to be built successfully, we must construct it within the tolerance of God's constraints. It is only by applying His dimensioning and adhering to His constraints that the full potential of the marriage can be released.

We can restate Matthew 19:8 another way - that divorce so defiles the product that it no longer adheres to the Manufacturer's design.

God is the one who declared the end from the beginning. It is He who made the blueprints, if you will, for the design of our lives. As the designer and creator, He created a space in our hearts. That place is meant by design for only God Himself to fill. It is only with Him occupying that place within us that we become endowed with the fullness of His power towards our maximum potential.

Filling that space with the comfort of a spouse or the fulfillment of a career is a recipe for difficulty, to say the least. No spouse, no job, no amount of money, no self-satisfaction, will ever live up to the promise of God within you!

Having completeness in Him empowers us to experience spouse, work, and our very lives to the full potential of His grand design. But let's not jump too far ahead here.

6. Preparing for the Call

I was on top of the world, and for the first time my whole life seemed on track . . . or was it?.

—ϻ—

There we were, members of Living Stone Cathedral of Worship. Senior Pastor Henry Hearns was more than a shepherd; he was like a spiritual father to us. It was under his leadership that our faith began to develop.

These were great times of learning, growing, and discovering a closeness with God which was never before considered a possibility. Friendships were built that would last a lifetime. We wanted to be used by God in any capacity He chose.

Within a few years of service there, Pastor Hearns asked if I would chair the church Board of Trustees, and I accepted. Soon Cozzette began serving by volunteering her time once per week to computerize the church's finances.

There were many church-related activities to get involved with. For certain, we got involved with as much as possible. We enjoyed it. We couldn't get enough church! The Power of God could be seen, and His presence could be felt there. I think one of the reasons we stayed so busy at church was a sense of great accomplishment that came from being part of something *God* was doing.

And faith was all we talked about. Our lives were transformed from being shrieking outsiders, to functional members of His body. Neither of us imagined that we could or would ever be people of significance within a church!

Professionally, the thought of a ministry vocation was little more than a fantasy. "It would be nice if my life were different," I thought, whenever I pondered the idea of doing any type of full-time ministry.

The thought of earning a living at ministry seemed impossible. We were raising Barry Jr. and had many financial obligations. We had grown into a lifestyle that demanded financial security. Neither of us could picture ourselves in a ministry vocation.

To sum up my career to that point, I was a "techno-geek" who hated to read anything other than technical manuals, blueprints, and service bulletins. I loved to solve complex problems, and enjoyed the challenges of figuring mechanical things out.

From drawing board to practical living, my life wasn't much different. Cozzette would joke that I needed a drawing board to figure out certain social skills. When she did, I would just chuckle, presuming it was some sort of endorsement of my intellect.

Faith was an interesting puzzle. It didn't fit into Ohm's Law or Brunelli's equations. It expected me to do something that was extremely uncomfortable – trust in something I couldn't measure with the senses, layout on the drawing board, or build with my hands.

Yet, something happened at that church in Littlerock that neither of us expected. Our faith began to grow. Not that all of our problems were solved overnight – they weren't. Yet we began to see God's hand in our present situations. And with us watching, He chose to show us a consistency, which could not be measured by formula, explained logically, or forged through cunning craftsmanship. We began to honestly know that God is real.

Time prohibits at this point going into the litany of testimonies I could give here. The bottom line is, that as we began to seek Him, God began making Himself known to us in often-inexpressible ways. This knowledge of Him was as certain to us as any of the laws of physics. In fact, the closer we drew to Him, the more we understood that He is more reliable than the best logic or technology humankind could ever conceive.

Faith became a staple in our lives. Service to God became our desire.

Business at our computer store had its share of "ups and downs." With the onset of the L.A. Riots, which came in the wake of the Rodney King beating, the economic face of Los Angeles changed dramatically.

We were feeling the heat. Large contracts where we supplied fortune 500 companies with computer technology evaporated, as those companies relocated or were otherwise affected by the riots.

Physically, our business escaped the trashing mobs that acted out their rage during an indiscriminate night of civil unrest. Economically, things got very tight, very fast. Though times became difficult, we trusted that God would bring us through, and He did.

It was during this time of financial struggle that we decided to take our walk with God to new levels by letting people know about our faith in Him. We began to share Christ with customers who patronized us. Those who called our store on the phone heard Christian radio whenever they were placed on hold. No question, we were taking a decisive stand in proclamation of our faith.

What we experienced next is what I believe every believer experiences as he or she begins to make a stand for Christ

– abandonment. People we once drank and "partied" with now found us contemptible. For the most part, this included our business relationships.

That's not to say that I'm making any justification for the methods we employed in making that stand – I'm not. In hindsight, there was any number of ways our public "declaration for Christ" could have been handled in a more loving way.

What I am saying is that as Christians "come out from among" their former life-style, there is likely to be a "hiss" or two from those who would rather hold on to their self-destructive indulgences. Such was the case for us. The impact for us was more lost business.

Despite the consequences, we were determined to live, work, and do business in a "Christ-like" fashion. If we had learned anything, it was that we could trust God's word. The road we were on was changing. Almost suddenly the Rolls Royce we had our eyes on lost its allure.

As the pick-up truck Cozzette drove began to age, the need for another car became apparent. Yet, this time it didn't have to be a brand-new car. This time, we were not motivated by the things that once drove us. We soon found a slightly used Ford Explorer that could well handle this part of our journey.

My focus was changing, and so was Cozzette's. One verse of scripture resounded in our souls:

> *"For what profit is it to a man if he gains the whole world, and loses his own soul? Or what will a man give in exchange for his soul?" (Mat 16:26 NKJV)*

In light of this scripture, for some reason, our souls became important to us.

Peter was our friend, competitor, and business acquaintance. It took years to build a relationship with him. Nothing appeared to affect Peter's computer business. The economic upheaval churning in the wake of L.A. riots did not seem to slow him down.

When we first met Peter, it didn't matter to us that he had an altar in his store upon which he sacrificed fruit to idols. When we needed help, Peter was there. He would often give us ten to fifty thousand dollars in computer merchandize to sell at the computer shows, and trust us to settle our account within the next month.

One day we tried to share our newfound faith with Peter. Peter didn't seem to mind our faith, yet he would rather talk about business than religion. "When you're as successful as I am, then you can talk to me about your religion," he said.

When Cozzette and I got back to our office, I noticed there were some tears streaming down her face. When I asked what was wrong, she said that Peter's statement upset her. "How long will God allow an idol worshipper to mock us?" She said. I felt it too. It was a profound sense of injustice that God's own so struggled while the idolater appeared to prosper.

Again, we found comfort in the scriptures.

"Let the lowly brother glory in his exaltation, but the rich in his humiliation, because as a flower of the field he will pass away. For no sooner has the sun risen with a burning heat than it withers the grass; its flower falls, and its beautiful appearance perishes. So the rich man also will fade away in his pursuits." (James 1:9-11 NKJV)

Not that we didn't wish Peter well. But our computer business was suffering while Peter's appeared to prosper. It just didn't seem fair. Little did we know that God was nudging us into a different direction, little did we know that He was making ready His call.

The confirmations that God was doing something different in our lives were mounting, and the Lord began teaching us to hear His voice.

As the Lord ministered to us through various testimonies; we were excited to share with others about lessons we learned. One evening we were at Baker's Square Restaurant in Palmdale. It was late and we were ministering to another couple over dinner about how we were learning to hear and trust God.

I shared with them how, one day on the way back to my office in Van Nuys, while in traffic on Victory Boulevard, the Lord impressed upon me to give a ride to the next person who approached the car. I told them how immediately after sensing the Lord telling me this, a man knocked on the window of the car. When I rolled the window down, the man asked for a lift. He was a bit gruff in appearance, but he had a quiet countenance.

He got in the car, and, as I began to drive him, this man said that he was involved in ministry and needed a ride to a local church. He gave directions as I drove, and oddly enough, the church he was headed to was only a few blocks away. He thanked me for the ride and then I just couldn't see where he went.

As I told this story that night, there came a unique sense that God was about to confirm this testimony to this couple by doing it right there again.

We finished our dinner and were about to get into the car to drive this couple home. By this time, I was positive that God was telling me once again to give the next person that approached us a ride to wherever he needed to go.

I was ready that evening to do whatever the Lord said to do. I was concerned, however, for Cozzette, and felt that she might feel vulnerable picking up a stranger. We had this couple with us that had to be taken home first, and we had

Barry Jr. with us as well. Nevertheless, there was a certainty that we were safe in God's leading.

Seeing the man crossing the street towards us, I turned back to Cozzette and said, "Cozzette, He's doing it again, God just told me that this man will ask us for a ride and we are to give it to him."

As I finished talking, the man came over and immediately asked for a ride to Lakeview Terrace. For those of you who don't know, Lakeview Terrace would be about an hour's drive away. In addition, it was going to take an hour to drive the couple we were ministering to home and get back to the freeway. Then, of course, was the hour's drive home again. Given the lateness, we knew that it would be about 1 A.M. before we got back home.

We trusted in what God was saying and loaded everyone into the Ford Explorer. As we drove this couple home, the man we were giving the ride to began to tell us that he was a "street preacher." He went on to say how he has ministered all across the nation. He told us how much he loved to proclaim the Gospel of Christ.

The drive down to Lakeview Terrace seemed almost surreal. Inside the car there seemed a dim but noticeable iridescent bluish-grey glow along with an incredible weightiness of peace, as this man ministered verbatim scripture upon scripture. Outside, there was an unseasonable fog cover, the heaviest I had ever seen on that stretch of Highway 14. It was a mid-summer night in the dry desert community. There was no rain, the weather had been clear and hot, but this night, the fog engulfed us, and for a while appeared to be holding us captive.

As we drew near to Lakeview Terrace, the fog lifted. The man had us drive around for a while as if he were trying to find a particular place for us to let him out. "There it is," he shouted and pointed to a huge empty paved lot. There were no buildings in sight, just this abandoned lot. "Are you sure?" I asked. "I can get the rest of the way from here," the man answered.

Before he opened the door to get out of the car, he said, "You did well by not forgetting the scripture." With that he quoted this verse:

> *"Do not forget to entertain strangers, for by so doing some have unwittingly entertained angels."* (Heb 13:2 NKJV)

Then he said, "I won't see you again on this side, but I will see you in heaven."

As he exited the car, I said to Cozzette, "Keep watching him, I want you to see exactly where he goes." Just then the man was gone. We did not see him vanish, but we saw him walking towards the center of this lot, then suddenly he was gone, and there was no place he could have gotten to, it was a vacant lot. We were watching him intently, and then we saw him no more.

There comes a time in the surrender to God's leading when you know that it's just time to "let go" and trust God. It's like learning to ride a bicycle. At first you have training wheels. Then your parents begin to move the training wheels ever slightly upward. You feel yourself doing it, then the wind blows and you rest to either side, leaning again to the training wheel. Then one day your parents bring you outside only to discover that the training wheels have been taken off altogether.

With this experience there came a sense that God was "raising the bar," and I would soon be unable to lean to my own understanding, take my own road, or pursue my chosen vocation. Instead I had to begin giving serious consideration to making an election for the call of God.

These testimonies, these lessons, these truths came at a time when I was pondering God's call into ministry. God has a way of so touching each person in the complexity of their thoughts. There He establishes His sovereignty with a unique, individual, and personal touch. His leading is so tailored to our lives that, if we are paying attention, it becomes undeniable.

God's call was more real than anything I had ever experienced. Its proof was in the overwhelming confirmations He gave through many personal testimonies.

The fact that God was calling was apparent, what was not yet evident was whether or not I would answer. Before we go further, let's go back and look at the call itself.

7. The Call

*Still, there was no getting around the fact
that God was calling my promise due.*

—ɷ—

Over a year had passed since the L.A. Riots, and business
hadn't recovered. We laid off most of our staff, and
were still hopeful that our business would "bounce back."
By my estimation, the business should have folded already.
Yet, somehow we kept going.

Spiritually, things had never been so good. We were
recognized leaders in our church, and were holding to the
confidence that God would help us through.

By September of '93 we realized that the business needed
financial help, so I fell back on my Aircraft Design skills,
and took a job with Burns Aircraft in Los Angeles.

Feeling a hint of discouragement one evening, I began
to study my Bible. Not that I was in any way attempting
to escape. Quite the contrary—my experiences with God
proved that there is safety nearest Him in any storm. And so
I retreated to my home office for a time of devotion, study,
and prayer.

That's when I heard it. It was as though someone was
audibly speaking; yet I was (apparently) alone in the room.

I heard it all at once, though I understood it as someone speaking. It was my calling.

Immediately I knew that the Lord most High, the God of all creation, had called me to pastor. "Why me?" I cried. "Why not you?" He said. "You promised that you would do whatever I asked."

Certainly, I didn't expect God to take that prayer so literally! After all, I'm just this "techno-geek" who owned a computer business and helped out at church! What did I know about being a pastor? It all seemed too fantastic, too impossible.

For the next week, I kept silent about this experience. During that time, all I honestly wanted to do was cry. The implications were a bit overwhelming. The impact upon my hopes, dreams, and ambitions seemed profound. And so for a week, while I wrestled with these thoughts, the inner controversies of my dreams were confronted by His will.

After that time, I discussed the call with Cozzette, and she cried for a week.

Shrewd businessman that I was, my response to God's calling was to attempt to strike a deal. "When I hear others tell me what I heard You say, then I'll know it was You and I will pastor," I said. Somehow my logical mind estimated the odds of someone actually repeating to me what I heard from God, as beyond reason. And so I took comfort in the thought that it could be many, many years, if ever, I would be obligated to pastor.

The next day we were at a church function, when Pastor Hearns' brother Doug, came over to me and said, "How ya doin' preacher?" Goose bumps – That's the only way to describe how I felt. "But that's not word-for-word what You said," I looked toward the sky as I said.

Cozzette and I were both determined that no one would know about our calling. It was our secret, or so we thought. Over the next two years, even strangers approached me calling me "preacher." None of them spelled it out the way I heard it from God though, and this was my excuse to keep running from the call.

Towards the end of '95, there came a strong sense that the Lord was about tired of my disobedience. It was nearing Christmas time and Cozzette and I decided to go to the Northridge Mall for some shopping. We entered from the second floor parking lot through the food court. On the drive down from Palmdale, I had a strong sense that the Lord was questioning my readiness to pursue His calling.

The Mall was so crowded that you couldn't see more than a couple of feet in front of you. Suddenly, the background noise faded, and it seemed as though the crowd parted to reveal a man sitting alone in a wheelchair.

Whether he was perched under some mall light or not, I don't know. All I know is that for some reason this man stood out and there was a clear path in the crowd between him and us. "Go lay your hands upon him and tell him to get out of that chair as you proclaim the name of Christ," I heard this voice say. It was as distinct as the day I heard the calling.

Immediately, my heart filled with fear at the thought of all the "what ifs." What if he doesn't get up and walk? What if he gets mad? What if he *really does* get up? Shameful fear. In response to God's urging me to pray for this man, I bargained again with God. "If that man comes over to me and talks to me, then I will know it was You Lord, and I will do what you ask." I prayed.

Immediately the man became lost from my sight as the crowd encroached upon the pathway between him and us. The man disappeared from sight, and there came a relief as I concluded a bargain had once again been struck with God. After all, what are the odds of running into that man again? And, if so, what were the odds of him actually coming over to speak to me? I felt pretty safe.

Several hours went by. We were tired and ready to go home. I could feel a tugging on my pant leg as someone pushed his way through the crowd. "Excuse me sir, can you show me the way up?" I turned and saw that same man, the one I saw earlier, of whom the Lord spoke to go and lay my hands on. "Can you show me the way up?" he said again.

My reaction was somewhat reminiscent of Jackie Gleason when he was caught speechless. "Hamnana, humnana, humnana." I was petrified. At once I was filled with both fear and the knowledge that I was trying to out-maneuver God.

Both with respect to my calling and this present situation, I (wrongly) assumed that if I could somehow make the requirements difficult enough, God would not be able to accomplish it, and I would be "off the hook." But now I felt caught red-handed in my schemes by the almighty God Himself, before Whom all my ways lie naked and exposed.

The rest is frankly a testament to my shame. I gave that man directions to the elevator, but remained too fearful to lay my hands on him.

What I experienced after that can only be described as incredible grief. It was something I never experienced before, a soul-wrenching grief that was extremely uncomfortable. Just as sure as I knew that power = amps X voltage, or that the area of a circle is pi times radius squared, I knew that, had I been obedient, that man would have walked. It was as if I knew that God wanted that man to walk, but He wanted it to happen through me. For the first time, I saw my disobedience to God's call adversely affecting someone else's life. The pain of that knowledge was almost more than I could bear.

A few weeks later our church was concluding an annual fast. We were to come together for prayer at the church, then break the fast together. This particular year, Cozzette and I drove to church to break our fast together with several ministers. While on that long road between Palmdale and

Littlerock, the car suddenly got quiet. "Barry," one of the ministers said, "do you know what your calling is?" One could hear a pin drop in the car. Cozzette and I just looked at each other in bewilderment. "Yes." I replied. This minister didn't say anything else about it.

"Do you know what my calling is?" I asked her. "Yes," this minister said, and she began to give it word-for-word as the Lord gave it to me some two years earlier.

In the weeks to follow, there was one Saturday night when I was awakened about eleven o'clock in the evening. There it was, it was His voice again, "Your Pastor does not have a message for tomorrow. Prepare a message that you will deliver to the congregation." I wanted to "make another deal" with God so I wouldn't have to bring the message. But, I reasoned that it didn't hurt to prepare a message, even if I didn't do anything but bring it with me "just in case." This was a frightening proposition. I had never delivered a sermon before.

By two A.M. the message was finished when I heard Him say, "Now call your Pastor and let him know you have the message for tomorrow." "Lord, if I get to church tomorrow and Pastor Hearns says he does not have the message, then I will know I heard from you, and I will be ready to bring the message," I replied in prayer.

I suppose that my insecurities kept me from obedience. After all, nobody knew me as a Pastor, or even a minister.

Within our church social climate, a few (in my estimation) only came to church for personal gain. There was, at some level, backbiting as ambitious people sought to "cut down" others in order to exert their right to a position in the "pastor's court." Sickening, but nonetheless this was a reality in the dynamic that existed at church at that time.

The fact is that some people already resented my position as Chairman of the Board of Trustees as well as whatever favor I had with Pastor Hearns. They were verbal about it. Announcing to the church that I have been called to Pastor would have had implications tantamount to being thrown into the pit. Still, I made a promise to God that I would do whatever He called me to do.

Until now some promises I made to God were casually kept. Whatever conditions I imposed upon those agreements were a vain attempt to out-maneuver God. It was a subtle reluctance to proclaim outwardly the fullness of faith which was developing inwardly. In response, God measured His grace towards me, in that He allowed me to deal with whatever insecurities spawned that reluctance. But now there was no getting around the fact that God was calling *my* promise due.

As he rose to the pulpit the next morning, Pastor Hearns' first words were, "I don't have a message for you this morning!" As I reached for the message which was prepared in my coat pocket, Pastor went on to say, "Jesse Osborne will bring the message today." A ram in the bush saved me!

After the service, I asked Pastor Hearns if he was awake at eleven o'clock the previous evening. His countenance became very solemn. "Eleven o'clock and again at two o'clock.!" he answered quite pointedly. After that I shared with him how the Lord called me to preach and Pastor Hearns confirmed that I did in fact hear from the Lord. He licensed me to preach not too long after that, though while I remained a member of his church, I never shared with him the whole of my calling.

8. Reflections

This was to be a defining moment in our marriage.

—◊—

S omewhere between the L.A. riots and accepting the calling came the Northridge Quake that decimated the face of the San Fernando Valley. Miraculously our business was not looted, despite the fact that the earthquake shook the front door of our computer store off its hinges. Yet the economic conditions following the earthquake caused us to eventually shut our computer business down. The damage was too widespread, and we just couldn't hold on till things picked back up.

In the months before we closed our business, I went to work for Burns Aircraft. By then my paycheck was helping to keep our business afloat. Eventually my work completed at Burns Aircraft and I was laid off. In April of '94 we were faced with making one of the toughest decisions we had to make as a couple. We could no longer pay the rent on our storefront. Several years of building, several years of dreams had come to an end as we closed our doors.

For nine months I looked for work and found none. Our savings were exhausted. If I were to try to explain how we

71

managed through that season, it would be impossible. We had no income with which to pay our mortgage, buy groceries, or even buy gasoline with which to get to church.

Yet, though slightly overweight, during this lean time, neither of us lost a pound. By the unexplainable grace of God, we always had, to the penny, exactly what we needed from day to day.

By the ninth month of looking for work, Cozzette and I were beginning to think that we may have to forfeit our home and perhaps relocate to a town with more job openings.

Late one evening, while sitting at my desk at home, I received a call from Mother. To set the scene for this call, I need to give some background.

We were not raised religious in any manner. During the years following my own conversion, there was much time spent in prayer and hope that the rest of my family would come to Christ. God answered that prayer, still as a family we had many hurdles to overcome.

Back home, in the Bronx, during the seventies, there were some turbulent times both within and without. Life was a matter of survival, and my family was no different. We each sought our own way of coping; each found our own pace in learning and growing.

For years, I buried myself in studies and music, excelling scholastically and progressing at a fledgling musical career. Ironically, though I excelled in these areas, I was extremely naïve. In fact, perhaps the majority of my contemporaries excelled beyond me in terms of "street smarts," which was a valuable commodity in Fort Apache.

Be that as it may, by my teenage years, I surrendered to the call of the "streets," and for a season attempted to "catch up" on the street life I thought I'd missed. Eventually, I became drunk with a near lethal cocktail of youthful exuberance, indulgence, and ignorance. In response to the external pressures, I compromised; in response to the internal pressures, I escaped.

Having unresolved issues, time stood still when I got on that plane to leave New York and my family back home.

For almost the next thirty years, our memories of each other would be filtered by the climate of that era, and the season in which I left home.

One of the legacies of "flight" are missed opportunities. When we run from pressures we take an unresolved road. It's like going "off roading." It may seem fun for a little while, but you're not getting very far and you're not going that fast. Eventually your body becomes fatigued by the trauma of the ride.

It's far better to take the "paved road," even though you may hit a few bumps, once you get beyond them, you get to your destination a whole lot quicker, easier, and safer.

My dear friend and fellow laborer in the Lord, Dr. Robert Colwell once said," We all come from the same polluted pool." What he meant by that is that all of us are imperfect and come from imperfect backgrounds. The person we "bring forward" will carry the aroma of the world and the pressures left behind.

It was nearly six years after boarding that plane from New York when Cozzette and I married. In the void of great time and distance, my family at home saw only the troubled youth who left home, and the failed marriage as an adult. They had no reason to trust in my decision-making; neither did they know the Christ who was at work in me. Consequently, they were reluctant to "get close" to Cozzette.

But time and grace had ministered many invaluable lessons. Lesson one: it is more important to be "whole" in the Lord than half with a spouse. With God, one plus one equals one, which is to say that one whole individual joined in marriage with one whole individual becomes one in Christ. A person whose heart is not whole by virtue of the brokenness of an unresolved past can not offer a whole heart to a spouse or to God.

This is the "baggage" we carry from the "polluted pool" of our past. The effects of a heart left broken are corrosive. And its corrosive properties erode away wherever it is damaged. If in love, then love it will invade. If in faithfulness, then to fear will it give rise. And if the heart was broken in passion, then the corrosion of complacency will erode the soul.

Lesson two: God hates divorce. In years of pasturing, I've heard much rambling from eroded hearts.

We have an adversary whose primary tactics have not changed throughout the ages, and whose primary weapon is deceit. He works by presentation of false reports, luring the unsuspecting away from the Truth.

In the Garden, his lies seduced Eve and captured Adam. In marriages today, he attempts to convince people that they are either somehow "missing out" on something or suffering unduly. Yet the biggest lie of all with respect to marriages, the biggest hoax perpetrated upon God's holy covenant, is that divorce will bring "closure." Divorce never brings closure; it tears at the lives of not only the broken couple, but their families, friends, and communities. And its tearing is violent and perpetual.

> *"'For the LORD God of Israel says that He hates divorce, For it covers one's garment with violence,' Says the LORD of hosts. Therefore take heed to your spirit, That you do not deal treacherously." (Mal 2:16 NKJV)*

My failure at marriage further fractioned relationships with my family back home. As a result, they were more reluctant to get close to Cozzette. Whether knowingly or unknowingly, this made Cozzette feel like an "outsider."

Lesson three: Leave and cleave. This was a lesson that presented me with many challenges. I knew that there were still unresolved issues that required healing and reconciliation with my family back home. Yet my wife needed to know that she would never be second, not to my past, not to my future, not to my family.

This is not a lesson in insecurity; it's a lesson in godly obedience. Our spouses must come first in our lives, with respect to all others, second only to God. It is only in this proper framework that empowerment and life-giving properties are released into our marriages.

Failure to establish safe and proper boundaries to protect your spouse can set up the groundwork for tension, hurdles, and even disaster.

This was a difficult hurdle for Cozzette and me, which culminated with Mother's call.

In the early years of marriage, when at times we had financial stress and the family wanted me to visit, they would send only one airline ticket. This meant that if Cozzette wanted to go with me she was expected to "find money for her own ticket."

On the surface this may appear as "no big deal." But beneath the surface the undercurrent was a subtle reluctance to fully embrace Cozzette as part of the family. The message was clear. To my family, Cozzette and I were not one. I was family and she was an "outsider."

To say the least, this was tremendously hurtful to Cozzette. What compounded her hurt was my own failure to ensure that no one came between us, not even my own family.

Thanks be to God for Pastor Colwell, whose ministry to marriages helped me to identify my own "baggage," and brought the scripture to life:

"And He answered and said to them, 'Have you not read that He who made them at the beginning 'made them male and female,' and said, 'For this reason a man shall leave his father and mother and be joined to his wife, and the two shall become one flesh?' So then, they are no longer two but one flesh. Therefore **what God has joined together,** *let not man separate." (Mat 19:4-6 NKJV)*

What follows is a "momentary light affliction." It is not about disrespect or dishonor. It is about caring enough to stand on His word, and having faith to trust God for the restoration.

When Mom's call came, as I had been out of work for nine months, our savings were exhausted, and we had no foreseeable means of paying our mortgage or even buying groceries, the stage was set. This was to be a defining moment in our marriage.

The customary greetings were exchanged when Mother mentioned that my brother Kenneth was getting married. She said that the wedding was to take place in Texas, and, of course, the family was sending me a ticket.

Cozzette and I were broke. We had no means of buying a plane ticket for either of us. Yet, the family insisted that they would only pay for my ticket, and a ticket for Barry Jr..

As lovingly as I could, I let Mother know that my love for my brother is deep and sincere. I wanted to be there for his wedding, but if the family were to exclude sending a plane ticket for my wife on this occasion, I would regretfully have to decline.

After explaining that I had to consider my wife's heart, I told Mom that this is something we would earnestly take to prayer. "Mom, I promise you I will pray, but my wife and I are one. I believe that if God wants me to be there at Kenneth's wedding, we will both be there." Mother couldn't at that time understand my position. But I trusted God to make a way for us to be at my brother's wedding and help Mom to understand.

As I recall it was the very next business day when the call came from a headhunter in Connecticut. After nine months of not being able to find a job, this recruiter explained that Weber Aircraft was looking for someone to start immediately. They wanted someone with exactly my experience. "Where's the job?" I asked. "Just north of Dallas, Texas in Gainesville," he replied.

Why it took nine months for prayers regarding employment is not something I want to discuss here. But I think it would be hard to deny the "hand of God" in the swiftness between that phone call with Mother, the resulting prayer, and this job offer for work in the same vicinity as my brother's wedding!

And so I called Mother back and asked her to go ahead and send me that plane ticket. How else was I going to get to Texas for this job?

By the end of my second week at Weber, I received a request to interview for a job back at Edwards Air Force Base, not too far from my home in California. Computer Sciences Corporation (CSC) paid for a round trip back home to California in order for me to be present for this interview. I went to this interview and returned to my hotel in Texas for work.

It was about a week after my interview with CSC that I decided to use Mother's return trip ticket. The paychecks from Weber were pretty good, and I had raised enough money to go home to California, pick up my car and drive Cozzette and Barry Jr. to Texas.

We checked into our new hotel upon our arrival in Texas, and within a few minutes there was a knock on the door. It was the Fed Ex deliveryman. He came to deliver my job offer to work at CSC back at Edwards. How we were at this particular hotel at the precise moment the job offer came in was beyond me.

Cozzette reminds me that I gave the updated hotel information for where we were going to be to the folks at CSC. Though we never did check into *that* hotel, CSC, by mistake, used the address for the former hotel, which I stayed in prior to this. As it turns out, the new hotel was not acceptable, and we checked into my old hotel. And as we sat there, having just walked into the room, we were discussing that I needed to call CSC and update them with the hotel information. It was at that moment that Fed Ex knocked on the door with the job offer!

So here we were, one job offer in hand for work starting in two weeks right near our home in California. And at the same time there was this great paying job right in Texas where my brother was getting married. Cozzette, Barry Jr., and I were all together in Texas. We had our car, a great paycheck, and Brother's wedding was in one week.

When we showed up at Brother's wedding together, Mother looked at me in amazement. "Remember how I told you I would pray?" I asked her. "Well, at this moment I have two jobs, and Cozzette and I are both here!"

And so having only worked in Texas for five weeks at Weber, my family and I were able to return to our home in California. It was five weeks whose outcome revealed new hope and new promise. It was a time, when for us, the waters parted and the road became visible before us.

God brought us by a mighty hand, He sent us out on a "round trip" journey, on a road called faith.

9. Returning Home

Yet through it all I gained a greater awareness of God.

—∿—

Work at CSC was somewhat rewarding. There were lots of computer "toys" to play with. By that I mean that there were a lot of challenging components and networks to configure.

Back at Living Stone Cathedral of Worship things were getting back to normal. It felt good to be back at our home church. And so I was back in my comfort zone – working to pay the bills while hiding from my calling.

Pastor Hearns had me bring the message as a minister on a few occasions, but the thought of becoming a Pastor was still unsettling.

Within a few short years I became extremely discontent with my job at CSC, and began looking elsewhere.

I soon went to work for a local hospital as their Computer Network Manager. The money was good and I was able to retire the Nissan Maxima and buy a new full-sized Chevy Crew-Cab as well as trade the Explorer in on a late-model Oldsmobile mini-van. It was another perfect job, or so I thought.

The people seemed to love me. I was like the "golden child." They needed me to solve all their system problems, and I had all their answers. In fact, Human Resources and upper management felt I was so over-qualified for the Network Manager position, that promotion was inevitable. It was by no means an easy job. The work and the hours were grueling, but I loved it.

It was about the time that I came to work at this hospital that I had occasion to speak with an old friend from another computer business in the Northridge area. Both of us knew Peter well. "How's Peter?" I asked. "You mean you don't know?" he said. He went on to ask if I had seen the paper that day. As it turns out, the paper headlined "Peter Luk Indicted For Intel Robbery."

This is a sensitive subject for me. Peter was a dear friend. Yet at once, in addition to shock and grief, my mind was filled with the memories of how Peter offered fruit to idols upon an altar in his business. I remembered how Cozzette cried at the thought that we, God's servants, were losing our business, while this man appeared to prosper.

I make no indictment of Peter and do not claim to know the particulars in this case other than the spiritual implications, which have been discussed. I did marvel, however, at the way Cozzette and I once felt, that while our business was closing, Peter's flourished. We had no resentment or ill feelings regarding Peter's apparent success. Yet when our business was facing closure, we couldn't help but ask God why.

The news of Peter's troubles came at a time when Cozzette and I were beginning to prosper. For us, this lesson was enough to confirm God's will for His people. Yet the toughest news was about to come.

Several months after Peter was released from prison, Cozzette and I were in the Van Nuys area and called Peter's business to let him know we wanted to drop by and say hello. That's when we were told that shortly after Peter was released from prison and returned to work, he was killed in a violent car accident.

I shall always miss Peter. And as I do, I wonder if I did enough to minister the Gospel to him. I wonder if someone in prison brought him to the Lord, I wonder if he ever had a conversion. And as I wonder, my passion is re-kindled to preach the Gospel of the Kingdom.

I suppose that my feelings about this whole situation can be summed up in Psalms 73.

"Truly God is good to Israel, to such as are pure in heart. But as for me, my feet had almost stumbled; My steps had nearly slipped. For I was envious of the boastful, when I saw the prosperity of the wicked. For there are no pangs in their death, but their strength is firm. They are not in trouble as other men, nor are they plagued like other men. Therefore pride serves as their necklace; Violence covers them like a garment. Their eyes bulge with abundance; They have more than heart could wish. They scoff and speak wickedly concerning oppression; They speak loftily. They set their mouth against the heavens, and their tongue walks through the earth. Therefore his people return here, and waters of a full cup are drained by them. And they say, 'How does God know? And is there knowledge in the Most High?' Behold, these are the ungodly, Who are always at ease; They increase in riches. Surely I have cleansed my heart in vain, and washed my hands in innocence. For all day long I have been plagued, and chastened every morning. If I had said, 'I will speak thus,' Behold, I would have been untrue to the generation of Your children. When I thought how to understand this, it was too painful for me; Until I went into the sanctuary of God; Then I understood their end. Surely You set them in slippery

places; You cast them down to destruction. Oh, how they are brought to desolation, as in a moment! They are utterly consumed with terrors. As a dream when one awakes, so, Lord, when You awake, You shall despise their image. Thus my heart was grieved, and I was vexed in my mind. I was so foolish and igno-rant; I was like a beast before You. Nevertheless I am continually with You; You hold me by my right hand. You will guide me with Your counsel, And after-ward receive me to glory. Whom have I in heaven but You? And there is none upon earth that I desire besides You. My flesh and my heart fail; But God is the strength of my heart and my portion forever. For indeed, those who are far from You shall perish; You have destroyed all those who desert You for harlotry. But it is good for me to draw near to God; I have put my trust in the Lord GOD, that I may declare all Your works." (Psa 73 NKJV)

Peter was my friend and colleague. I had love and respect for him. Yet through it all, I gained a greater awareness of God.

10. Dealing With Discouragement and Promise

The whole situation made me feel like a failure, no matter how much money we made. "How could God ever use such a failure?" I often wondered.

—⟋⟍⟋—

S hortly after I went to work for the hospital, Cozzette went to work for Children's Services.

So here we were, both Cozzette and I working at fairly decent jobs. We had new cars and experienced a financial freedom we had not previously known. Barry Jr. was in his last year of high school, and things overall were going pretty well for us.

The call to ministry was not completely gone from our minds, though it didn't seem that important at that time. We were finally enjoying a piece of the "American Dream."

The Lord called us out of Living Stone Cathedral of Worship, and we were serving in a small church in Lake Los Angeles. As far as ministry goes, we figured that if God wanted us to do ministry, He would have to provide a way for us to do it. Looking back, any thoughts of ministry at that point were secondary to our careers.

Not that we wouldn't do ministry, but that we couldn't imagine doing ministry in any way that would infringe on our jobs. We had answered the call to ministry by simply accepting preaching responsibilities, or so we thought.

In all the apparent splendor of the moment, there was a haunting overshadow. It was a pain that nagged at our every success. It was our desire to have a child of our own, together. For fourteen years, we had watched the Lord bless us in everything but our greatest desire. Barrenness foreshadowed everything. Whatever joy we had, it seemed as though our smiles were just an exercise in going through the motions.

Though I read about Sarah, Rebekah, Rachel, and Elizabeth, I never understood what the big deal was about barrenness. Yet now this subject was becoming painful for both of us. Admittedly, at first it didn't bother me so much. However, as the years rolled on, I began to feel Cozzette's pain.

It's a pain that can't be dismissed with a simple, "Well adopt a child." A pain you see in your wife's face after a miscarriage, and again every time she's asked, "How many children do you have?" The pain you both feel after a miscarriage when people say, "You shouldn't try any more," or "Maybe God doesn't want you to have children." It was a pain that could be felt in her tears and her solemn moments, as she wept countless times before the Lord.

If there was ever anyone who deserved to have a child, it was Cozzette. She lovingly gave of herself, despite her private pain, to raise a son, my son. And she did so with grace, love, and strength. She gave her all to him that was not hers.

We had faith, we had God, yet there was still this incredible feeling of un-fulfillment. There was something of significance missing.

In that atmosphere, there was a constant battle. It was a battle against thoughts and reminders of our own inadequacies. I would wonder if the reason for our barrenness was my own failed previous marriage. Perhaps God was punishing me for the failures of my youth. I sometimes wrongly felt that Cozzette's grief was a direct result of my divorce.

The whole situation made me feel like a failure no matter how much money we made or victories we won. "How could God ever use such a failure?" I often wondered. "Who would ever follow such a failure?" I thought. The "what ifs" were endless.

For the record, these thoughts were not from God. We know that in God there is restoration. This is more than just an issue of salvation. Jesus came to give us life, and life more abundantly. That's not simply a voucher for redemption in heaven – that's power for living here and now!

Our adversary knows how to turn discouragement to doubt. If we succumb to these tactics, we begin questioning God, questioning His Word, and questioning His calling. The irony is, these tactics haven't changed since the Garden of Eden.

"Then the serpent said to the woman, "You will not surely die. 'For God knows that in the day you eat of it your eyes will be opened, and you will be like God, knowing good and evil.'" (Gen 3:4-5 NKJV)

The adversary's tactics have not changed. It is enough of a slant, a distortion of the truth to bring about doubt in God's word, if we fall prey to it. All of us need to guard our hearts against such demonic tactics! To do this, we have to hold on to God's Word, in spite of our circumstances. We have to understand the value of remaining in His presence, through worship and the embrace of His Word.

We have an enemy that will use our every fault, our every failure in an attempt to persuade us that we are beyond God's redemption, restoration, or usefulness. That God would never desire to fulfill any promises in us, because our past has been tainted.

But God can and will use anybody. There is one prerequisite—that we make ourselves available for His use. His desire for us does not change because of our inadequacies. He desires that we come to Him and receive His promises.

> *"who desires all men to be saved and to come to the knowledge of the truth." (1 Tim 2:4 NKJV)*
> *"The Lord is not slack concerning His promise, as some count slackness, but is longsuffering toward us, not willing that any should perish but that all should come to repentance." (2 Pet 3:9 NKJV)*

God proved to me, through many confirmations, that we were called to pastor, and that we would have our child. Yet for the moment, neither seemed remotely possible. For the time being, His promise was all we had to hold on to.

In the wake of it all came a confidence and a boldness with which we can declare today that God can redeem and restore anybody.

11. What About Ministry?

*It was time to face reality and stop running
from the call.*

—ᴡᴡ—

Work at the hospital was fulfilling. The long hours and weekends kept me away from home often. There was a strong sense that I was being groomed at work for something more.

We referred to Wednesdays as "Marathon Meeting Wednesdays." Most Wednesdays were spent in meetings literally from sun-up to midnight. These were high-level meetings dealing with high visibility multi-million dollar projects. A success or failure in my work would inevitably be reported directly to the Board of Supervisors through one of these Marathon Meetings.

It was after one of these Marathon Meetings when I was at my "best game." Exhausted from the stringent meeting, I retired to my office. It was about eleven o'clock at night. I sat there leaning back in my chair with my feet up on the desk. "This is it," I thought. "White picket fence, new cars every year, it's all my dreams and hopes for success."

As I sat there pondering my success, there at once came a deep sense of neglect, along with a voice. "What about ministry?" I heard it just as loud and clear as if there were someone else in the room. I knew instantly the Lord was speaking to me.

"Well, I'm not sure how ministry is going to fit in with all this," I replied.

"What about ministry" I heard, resounding for the second time. "I guess once I'm successful enough, I'll do ministry," I answered.

For the third and final time I heard, "What about ministry?" This time I answered, "Lord, if you keep blessing me like this, I honestly don't know how I'm going to do ministry."

That night I left work with a strong sense that I had heard from the Lord, and that once again things were about to change.

What happened next is hard to explain. I suddenly fell out of favor at work. Where I once could do no wrong, I was now viewed quite differently. There were power struggles on every side, and I was in the middle.

The jobs that everyone felt I was being groomed for were given to people significantly less qualified in every dimension. And, without going into details or speaking ill of anyone, I became the focal point of abuse at the workplace.

Work was no longer fun. It became a nightmare. Where I once volunteered my time in pursuit of meaningful work progress, I was now forced to work long hours for no other reason than to satisfy someone's personal vendetta.

As a Christian, I felt compelled to give my best effort, despite the abuse. Yet, the effort I continued to give was a futile effort to satisfy a regime that could not be satisfied. I literally worked myself sick.

In the meanwhile, there came confirmation after confirmation that God wanted me to pastor. It was time to face reality and stop running from the call.

While sitting at the car wash one day, a man that I did not know came over and said, "You've got to stop running! God wants you to pastor!"

On another day, while driving home from visiting a friend, someone honked at me fearlessly. After I pulled over, a man jumped out that I had met on only about two occasions. This man is reported to have a prophetic gift. Though I had not seen him for quite some time, he exited his car, and while running towards me he began to shout, "God said it's time to stop running!"

Finally, I was at one of the hospital's satellite clinics, researching a system problem, when I ran into John Clarke. John had a fledgling ministry that he began several years earlier under the leadership of Pastor Hearns.

I hadn't seen John for several months. He mentioned that the Lord called him to another work in Laughlin, and that the Lord was sending someone to continue the work he began here.

John walked up to me that night and explained that he was only in town to see the doctor.

"Well, are you ready to quit running?" he asked. "Your ministry has been waiting for you!"

That night I knew that I had run out of excuses. I agreed to take on the ministry, and was installed as Pastor on October 10, 1999. The running was over, and after six years of running, I was ready to surrender to His call to ministry.

12. The Jacob Experience

God's church grew in spite of my plan, not because of it.

—ɯ—

My carnal mind reasoned that if God called me to pastor, it must be because of my management and business experience. I have since come to realize that God's most valuable asset in any of us is our willingness to follow His leading, not our own special talents or abilities.

In putting together a "church plan," I drew from engineering and management experience. This led me to quickly put together a "project plan," which had reasonable milestones enough to make the church successful in three years. I was confident in the call, and confident in my abilities to fill the call.

The church itself had no building, no checking account, no 501C(3), and the offerings were twenty-five dollars, when I put in twenty. There were a total of six people including my wife and myself. Only two of those original members came faithfully to service.

Surely, after finally finding such a good job, any plans for ministry would come second to my first vocation. And so my original plan was to devote myself to my full-time job, and give only part-time to the ministry until it grew. Sounds reasonable, doesn't it?

There was much work to be done. For a year we worked on "getting things in order" as the ministry grew to about twelve faithful.

Aaah. . . twelve, that's something to work with, and I knew exactly how these twelve would help to grow the ministry.

Everything seemed to be going well. Yet, there was this underlying sense that the Lord desired for me to put ministry first, and not the Job. It was as though I was supposed to walk away from the "dream job" in pursuit of full-time ministry.

In my heart, I felt that I was doing enough for God, that I was "on the road" to ministry, but I was determined to make that journey on my own terms. Ministry would be secondary, at least until I could build some kind of financial security.

Meanwhile, at work, things were heating up. To say that the workplace was becoming stressful would be a gross understatement. With a new regime came unfair and extremely abusive treatment.

At once, the long hours I enjoyed volunteering were now being demanded. Time prohibits discussing the litany of abuses brought in with the new regime. It's safe to say that the "dream job" became a nightmare.

My own personal failure at this point was in not under-standing the Lord's leading in my work situation. With all I had in me, I attempted to "rise to the challenge" by trying to please a boss that could not be pleased. I thought that, if I worked hard enough, and demonstrated my abilities, the new boss would come to appreciate my efforts.

But it was no longer about the work. It was no longer about the potential for personal career advancement manage-ment dangled before me. It was about the Lord saying, "Your season here is over, and it's time for your surrender."

That's when it began. Though previously my health was always pretty good, I suddenly found myself suffering from several seemingly unrelated medical problems. My hands were going numb, along with the entire left side of my body.

Frequent dizzy spells could not be diagnosed, no matter how many doctors I saw. Chronic bronchitis kept me returning to the doctor for medical treatment. I began having excruciating chronic pain several places in my body, and tremors that resembled Parkinson's Disease. I couldn't stop shaking. My body shook constantly as though it were frostbitten on a cold New York night, regardless of the temperature. And sleep, sleep was next to impossible.

But that wasn't the worst. The worst was a trembling, heart racing, uncontrollable, and unpredictable anxiety; it was a debilitating panic, when there was nothing wrong. There are few words to describe what these anxiety attacks were like, other than to say that I could feel adrenaline pumping relentlessly at all times. There seemed to be nothing I could do or take to control it. My doctors were at a loss. More important, it was not supposed to happen to *me*. After all, I'm a Christian!

Countless doctors were consulted. They could tell by my lab results that there was something wrong, but they couldn't figure out what it was.

Ironically, I wasn't about to let sickness keep me from meeting the impossible deadlines of my job, so I just pushed myself harder and kept going.

My complexion changed to a pale gray. Cozzette pleaded with me to stay home from work until I could find a doctor that could help. Well, the next doctor that I went to basically told me that if I stayed on my job, my wife needed to get ready to bury me. And so, I left computer work.

In the months that followed, my physical condition seemed to get worse. There were so many things going wrong, that I could not even explain to the doctors everything that was happening. I was pale, lethargic, and struggled to breathe. My waking moments were spent fighting this adrenaline rush, and I prayed for sleep that seldom ever came. My body shook from uncontrollable chills all the time.

"Why Lord?" I'd cry out as I lie on the sofa, lacking even the strength to go to my bedroom upstairs. "How am I going to build Your church like this?"

I was perplexed at the thought that it wasn't until after finally accepting the call to pastor that this illness appeared to onset so violently.

Within a few months the diagnosis began to come in. Pneumonia and Chronic Obstructive Pulmonary Disease were on the top of the list.

I struggled on Sundays to go to church, and struggled to speak. Afterwards, I went home and collapsed where I remained almost literally until the next week.

Nothing the doctors gave me seemed to work. I had a distinct realization that I was on the verge of death. My blood oxygen levels kept dropping. A year went by and I was still fighting the pneumonia, still staggering into church on Sundays to preach, still going home to collapse.

There actually came a time when I knew, with certainty, that if I didn't continue fighting to live, my body would simply "give up the ghost." I was exhausted beyond endurance, and wanted to quit.

It was in that atmosphere that I made two phone calls. One call was to my mother in New York. I wanted her to understand how sick I was, and I explained that I didn't think I was going to make it. The other call was to Pastor Hearns. I had seen the Lord answer prayer for this man in remarkable ways in the past.

When He came to my home, Pastor Hearns looked in my eyes and said, "Boy, if you're going to die, you best do it behind a pulpit." He was an encouragement to me that day.

What I realized at that point, was that I was previously willing to serve God, but only as long as I did not have to "lay it all down." It was as if I were a soldier saying, "I'll wear the uniform, I'll do the drills, I'll even march with you—just as long I don't have to actually take a bullet."

Those simple words from Pastor Hearns made me realize that I must be willing to "fight to the death," that whether I lived or died, what breath I had was His, to use for His purpose, in His way.

Though my entire Christian walk up to that point had brought me to a place of faith, something died that day. Something *I thought* had already been crucified—self. What awakened was the realization that part of the Christian walk means dying to yourself *daily*.

From that day it was no longer, "Lord, heal me so that *I* can grow Your ministry." It became, "Lord, give me strength, that, with all my being, I may do Your will."

The difference is diametrically opposed. The former falsely presumes that one's abilities are essential to God. The latter makes one's self available for His direction.

Since then there came a slow recovery, but a recovery, nevertheless. Though my body never fully bounced back, I am no longer completely bed-ridden. With the Lord's help, I am, to some extent, able to "work around" physical limitations.

Medically, Cozzette and I had been seeking answers for years as to why the sudden onsets of anxiety. There had to be a reason why such an outgoing personality became so suddenly and severely stricken with these debilitating attacks. After much prayer and years of doctor's visits, we have come to understand that these are side affects from steroids found in the pulmonary medications prescribed for COPD.

Since becoming so gravely ill, I learned that many pastors endure major crisis in their lives before giving their lives totally to the call. It's a "last stand," where an encounter with

God causes a release of self-will and an acceptance of His will, as well as a total reliance on Him.

This was my "Jacob Experience." Even as Jacob initially relied on his cunning abilities rather than the Lord, Jacob reached an impasse where he wrestled with God. As a result, Jacob's side was smote, causing him to lean on a crutch, a constant reminder of his weakness and his need to lean on the Lord. That place where he wrestled with God became Jacob's place of surrender.

Likewise, my craftiness and skill deceived me into thinking that I could have God on my own terms. That somehow I could live life my own way, adding God in much the same way we add salt to our food. That my career and ambition could be the main course, and what I did for God was ancillary.

This life-style led me to an impasse, a wrestle between my flesh and God's will. And the limitations I now face in my flesh, the scars, are a constant reminder of my need to rely completely on Him. It is that thorn in my own side, even the very lungs I use to draw breath, that force me to confront the memory of how I "wrestled" with God.

No longer physically able to follow the grand "project plans" drawn up to grow the church, I felt helpless and inadequate. Yet, in the months that followed, during those times I lay helplessly ill, God's church grew in spite of my plan, not because of it.

13. Releasing Old Ways

Little took away that loneliness; it became
a pain all to itself.

—꿈—

My struggle back to health became the toughest struggle of my life. Several things came about as a direct result.

In the first place, there came an understanding, a sympathetic compassion for people who suffer with long-term illness. I don't know if many people have such compassion. For sure, prior to this experience, there was little within me.

A vast majority of people, at some level, are uncomfortable around those who are fighting serious or long-term illness. This is not much different within the Christian community. Many Christians are reluctant to "visit the sick _in_ their infirmity."

There is often a silent judgment that comes into play. It's a judgment that assumes the suffering party is in that condition because of an inherent sin, and that the illness is God's judgment. Or if not judgment, the sick person is often viewed as having a lack of faith. In either case, there is a tendency to shy away from the suffering person, as though either a personal lack of faith or God's judgments are contagious.

97

This whole rationale is ridiculous. As Christians, coming near to those who are most ill should be what we purpose to do!

It's easy to rationalize that when people are ill, they probably prefer to be left alone. It's easy to excuse ourselves from this responsibility. Perhaps there are some who would rather be left alone at such a time, yet I have found that a visit at precisely that time brings an element of comfort to relieve the suffering person.

Besides, regardless of what reasons we have for not visiting the sick, Jesus makes it clear that visiting the sick is part of our responsibility. As He describes the "separation of the sheep from the goats," Jesus talks about this very issue.

> *"Then the King will say to those on His right hand, 'Come, you blessed of My Father, inherit the kingdom prepared for you from the foundation of the world: for I was hungry and you gave Me food; I was thirsty and you gave Me drink; I was a stranger and you took Me in; I was naked and you clothed Me; I was sick and you visited Me; I was in prison and you came to Me.'" (Mat 25:34-36 NKJV)*

In the next few verses of scripture, Jesus mentions that not doing these things for each other is the same as not doing them for Him. The former are called sheep, and are accepted by Him, while the later are likened unto goats, and rejected. In the latter case, no amount of religious rhetoric suffices.

Is it enough to think that just giving a minimal effort here will suffice? Can we assume that, because we are members of a church that feeds the hungry, visits the sick and imprisoned, shelters the homeless, and clothes the naked, that membership in such a church meets the "spirit" of Christ's position on this subject? Why take that chance? Why not live rather, in an earnest attempt in pursuit of the "spirit" of Christ's concerns?

From my own experience, the peak of my illness brought about unbearable loneliness. My wife went to work every day, and I was alone in the house to suffer all by myself.

Little took away that loneliness; it became a pain all to itself.

One by one I called my closest friends, who often implied that my faith was failing, and that this was the reason for my suffering. This line of reasoning became an "out card" so that people did not have to deal with my illness or me. For the most part, they treated me as though whatever symptoms I had, be they spiritual or physical, they were a contagious plague that could be transmitted by merely speaking to me.

On the other hand, there were those who chose rather to "bait" me. Foreknowing my condition, they would ask how I was doing. If I answered honestly, I was given a lecture on how simply saying, "I wasn't feeling well" was in itself a lack of faith.

It's not my intention here to give a sweeping indictment of any person or group of people. There are tendencies that all of us have which need to be guarded against. It wasn't until I became so ill that I discovered that there existed within me these same fears and phobias. In a real sense, this illness shattered my own prejudices about illness and Christianity.

How many of us can honestly say where our faith will be if faced with such a test of endurance? Even Peter denied the Lord three times when faced at once with the ramifications of knowing Christ.

It's easy to maintain faith during a "spat" of illness. It's relatively easy to pray when you must endure that minor surgery or a short recovery time. What about when it's all on the line? What about when the discouragement and serious-ness of a long-term illness *prevent* you from praying?

When there's no strength left, and you begin to come to the realization that your life-long plans and dreams may all be curt short, who can say really where faith will be?

Paul makes an interesting comment on this subject:

"We then that are strong ought to bear the infirmities of the weak, and not to please ourselves." (Rom 15:1 KJV)

Though Paul makes reference here to our public meal plan, the implication still follows. Those who are strong are to help the ones who are weak.

At any time, there could be a number of circumstances where any of us finds ourselves in a long-term illness or battle. Being Christian does not exclude us from tribulation.

Being Christian should call us to a sense of *responsibility* towards one another. When we find that a brother or a sister is suffering, our response should be anger—not towards the person, but towards the principalities and powers that war against His body. As a result, we should become motivated to take whatever action necessary to help our friend.

Consider the friends of the paralytic:

"Then they came to Him, bringing a paralytic who was carried by four men. And when they could not come near Him because of the crowd, they uncovered the roof where He was. So when they had broken through, they let down the bed on which the paralytic was lying." (Mark 2:3-4 NKJV)

True friends. They gave no lecture to the paralytic about his faith! Their friend was in need, and they acted upon *their* faith! Knowing the paralytic did not have the strength to come before the presence of Christ for his own healing, these friends were willing to do whatever it took. They even went so far as to tear the roof off a home to lower their friend before the presence of Jesus. What faith!

This is fundamentally what our response needs to be in hearing that any friend is ill. There needs to be an indignation that causes us to act. That action plain, and simply, is intercession. We ought to be willing to do some work, to lift our sick friends in prayer, sharing with him or her benefits of *our* strength. We can do this by keeping him or her before the presence of the Lord, and by visits of encouragement.

We cannot ignore each other's suffering. We should, rather, understand that God has called us to a friendship that *endures* suffering.

> *"And if one member suffers, all the members suffer with it; or if one member is honored, all the members rejoice with it." (1 Cor 12:26 NKJV)*

14. Expectations of Life

Jesus set aside His own rights, even His
right to save Himself

—∾—

Perhaps loneliness was not entirely for nothing. By now, Barry Jr. had since left home in pursuit of a career in the military. When Cozzette went to work the house felt empty. In the loneliness of my infirmity, I realized that there was something missing—children.

For the first seventeen years of our marriage, Cozzette's goals of raising a family were unfulfilled. The pain of that barrenness was felt in all aspects of our life. Nothing escaped the heaviness of her pain.

After the first several months of my illness, Cozzette began to feel the ramifications. In my own vanity I presumed that her tears at night were from her weeping over my condition, but they weren't.

Coming to terms with my own restrictions was one thing. Watching Cozzette come to terms with the fact that her husband may not ever be able to give her a child, much less raise a child together with her, was for her unbearable.

Though she rose to the challenges of "taking up the slack" for my inabilities, I could see Cozzette's own private suffering. The clock was ticking, and we could see that, if I did recover, we would miss our window of opportunity to have children forever.

Lying down at night caused me a great deal of pain. Acid Reflux Disease caused my throat to burn when I lay down, while problems with chest congestion made it difficult to breathe. Most nights I slept in the La-Z-Boy chair wrapped in a blanket anointed with chest rub and surrounded by a litany of medications and herbal remedies.

From my view in that La-Z-Boy, I watched as Cozzette cried herself to sleep each night. Each night, I became more and more concerned about her plight. After Cozzette left for work each morning, while lying alone, I began to seek the Lord's healing for both of us.

It was then that I realized that I had done almost *nothing* to secure my wife's dream of having children. Knowing the science involved in our case, I had previously taken a "back seat." My attitude was that if it were something she wanted to do, she would have to take all the initiative to make doctors' appointments and so forth.

Not that I had any particular "macho" attitude, I worked for my dreams, and I felt she needed to work for hers.

Without blame assessment, we have to recognize this thought process as a by-product of the feminist movement. At the risk of alienating half of the readers, my upbringing *was* affected by the feminist movement—it's how I was taught. In our home, our family had an extreme feminist view. It was an anti-male, and anti - "anything that has the appearance of traditional male or female role or responsibility" view.

What this extremism translated to was a viewpoint that there are no distinct male or female roles, and therefore each "pulling his or her own weight" becomes the focal point of the marriage.

The need for the feminist movement was evident. Women in society were often viewed as lesser citizens. However, a by-product of this movement has caused men today to be *less* aware of their need to cultivate fulfillment in their wives.

Let me say it another way. This struggle to say that men and women are equal in every way ultimately caused the man to withdraw from his supportive role in some fundamentally essential ways.

I'm talking about going beyond the general support all of us expect, such as support with a career or family. But if I see my spouse as an equal cohabitant with no difference other than genitalia, than I am not likely to see her in terms of my responsibilities to impart life, "and life more abundantly."

Often, when counseling couples that are having difficulty, I find that, while she has become disillusioned with his role as a husband, he is upset that she is not "towing the line" financially and/or physically. That's not to mention the increasing number of men who feel that they should be able to stay at home at least half of the time while their wives support them.

There are a growing number of men who see a marriage as two working people. They look for the advantage of that second income as a means of the family reaching accomplishments more quickly. When the woman begins to feel unfulfilled or burned out and needs to rest or change jobs, the couple has a "train wreck." She sees that, to him, money is more important than she is, and he feels that she is not being responsible.

So then are things truly equal? According to scripture, men have the greater responsibility. We are responsible to help our wives grow and become all that God created in them. Whether that means career or child bearing is an individual issue. Her ability to earn an equitable salary does not mean that, if her salary *fails to* equal mine, that somehow she's at fault. My responsibility to God is to love her — not because of her income, but because she's my wife by covenant.

The Apostle Paul shows us as men that we have a greater responsibility.

> *"Husbands, love your wives, even as Christ also loved the church, and gave himself for it; That he might sanctify and cleanse it with the washing of water by the word, That he might present it to himself a glorious church, not having spot, or wrinkle, or any such thing; but that it should be holy and without blemish. So ought men to love their wives as their own bodies. He that loveth his wife loveth himself. For no man ever yet hated his own flesh; but nourisheth and cherisheth it, even as the Lord the church: For we are members of his body, of his flesh, and of his bones. For this cause shall a man leave his father and mother, and shall be joined unto his wife, and they two shall be one flesh. This is a great mystery: but I speak concerning Christ and the church. Nevertheless let every one of you in particular so love his wife even as himself; and the wife see that she reverence her husband." (Eph 5:25-33 KJV)*

As men we are instructed to love our wives "as Christ loved the church." Well, how did Christ love the church? Did He exalt Himself over it and demand silent submission from it? Of course not.

Jesus set aside His own rights, His right to save His life, and His right to pursue personal fulfillment. Instead, He endured hardship on our behalf. He came and met us at our point of need, and gave His own life for our sanctification and restoration.

Do we view our wives in terms of their responsibility to us? Or should we rather view our wives with an understanding of what our responsibility is to *them*? Clearly, the later is the scriptural viewpoint.

In hindsight, it's clear to see that the physical condition with which I was afflicted reflected my wife's emotional condition—dying and hopeless. It took coming near to death for me to realize that the failure was in not understanding my responsibility as a husband to cultivate life in my wife.

15. A Glimmer of Glory

*My meager steps towards meeting the
financial requirements were met with God's
supply.*

—⁓—

Admittedly, prior to my illness, there was an undercurrent, a feeling that I really didn't want to put forth the
effort of raising another child. I had two children, and they
were both grown. This was a sore spot in our marriage.

As I lay on the sofa each day in my private suffering, the
Lord began to minister to me that *I had failed* to bring life
to my wife's dreams. As her husband I had a *responsibility*
to help Cozzette find fulfillment, and not just seek my own.
If there was going to be life in this situation, it had to come
from me.

In the days that ensued, while I lie ill, I began to feel the
barrenness of an empty home. "If I were to die today, who
would grieve for me?" I wondered. It became painfully clear,
that what was missing in our home was children. And, for
the first time since our marriage, I truly wanted children.

It was perhaps my most difficult moments. Extremely
weak, I had been suffering from pneumonia for several
months. The doctors diagnosed me with Chronic Obstructive

Pulmonary Disease. They told me it was something I had to live with—if I lived at all. Every breath was a struggle.

One evening, after these diagnoses, when Cozzette came home, she looked at me and just began to weep horribly. I tried to comfort her and let her know I wasn't afraid to die. That's when I learned her tears were not for me. "You've accomplished everything you set out to do in your life, if you die now, I am unfulfilled, and that's not fair!"

Her life thus far had been a life of sacrifice. For all that we've been through, she was supportive and giving. She was there to help raise Barry Jr. She was there to run the computer store. When I became active in church leadership, Cozzette worked along side me. When it was time to pastor, she again put her dreams on hold and donned the role of a pastor's wife.

Yet there was a dream that she longed to see materialize, the one dream she prayed for all of her life. That dream was to find fulfillment in bearing and raising her children.

It was the thought of my mortality that increased the pain of her barrenness. It was all just too unfair. She had given into my fulfillment time and time again. From being an engineer's wife to the sacrificial life of a pastor's wife, Cozzette gave. And all the while, she was hoping and praying that God would hear her prayer and give her life.

I was not on this journey alone, and if I died I would not die on it alone. The career decisions I made brought requirements that were exacted from both of us, and it appeared as though Cozzette was about to be short-changed.

In light of my diagnosis, Cozzette had questions for God. She wondered if God would be so unfair as to bring us to His vocation, to bring us through so much, only to allow her dreams to die with me. Let's face it; neither of us was young anymore. The clock was winding down, and with each "tick" the sun was setting on her dreams, and there wouldn't be time for her to start over.

Suddenly none of my personal or private accomplishments mattered. I would have given up the house, the car, the careers, anything. Cozzette was desperately hurting, and she was *right*.

For medical reasons having a child for us was going to take considerable financial resources. I later sat down with Cozzette that night, and showed her how I was willing to make financial sacrifices to get a savings account going. Whatever initiative needed to be taken, I was willing to do it—sick or not. I had set my heart upon a purpose that I would have a child with my wife or die in the process.

The sacrifices I promised to make that night were faithfully kept. Slowly our savings grew to a few hundred dollars, then almost three thousand. What happened next was no less that a miracle. Time prohibits me from going into detail, other than to say that financial blessings poured in from unexpected places. Suddenly we had all the monies we needed for the medical procedure required to have our child.

Clearly, taking the responsibility for my wife's fulfillment created a pathway for life to flow from God. My meager steps towards meeting the financial requirements were met with God's supply.

A tremendous hurdle had been overcome, but I was still severely ill. I was physically in the worst condition of my life, and the prognosis was not good. I struggled for every breath, knowing that any single breath could be my last. I felt as though I were living on the verge of death. Cozzette felt I was, too.

Could God bring forth life from such a dead situation? Would He? If there was any hope of us having children, it was in the promises of our God, and not the hands of a doctor.

It had been the longest night of our lives. We were squarely on the right road now. It was the only true road, the road of God's choosing. And though the dawn was far beyond us, we began to see a glimmer of life that can only be found in complete surrender to the Lord of Glory.

16. Confirmation of Life

But, we were not motivated by logic, we were driven by faith and hope in the promises of God.

—᙮᙮—

By now we had nearly all the money we needed to have the medical procedure necessary for an attempt to have our child. It was a few weeks before taking that step that I attended my first "School of Pastoral Nurture" (SPN) class with Dr. Jack Hayford.

Five years earlier, the Lord spoke clearly to me that I was to "get under Jack Hayford." When I heard the Lord tell me this, I did not at the time know how or when to study under Pastor Jack. In fact, when I heard the Lord's voice on this subject, I was not yet a pastor, and one of the prerequisites of this class was that you had to be a pastor or have your pastor's recommendation.

So, here we were, pasturing a church publicly, and privately getting ready to give life to a life-long dream. Suddenly it looked as if Cozzette's fulfillment and my own fulfillment were in unison.

There was a longing in my soul to obey the voice of the Lord and begin my studies with Pastor Jack. Though still struggling with severe health issues I signed up for this SPN, not knowing if I was going to be well enough to complete a full week in a classroom setting.

As I sat there on the first day, Pastor Jack shared how five years earlier the Lord told him to start this School of Pastoral Nurture. There was no question in my mind that my being there at that precise moment was a "divine appointment."

As the week went on, Pastor Jack shared his views on the husband and wife relationship. "Life flows from the man," Pastor Jack went on to say. Listening gave me goose bumps. It was a concise confirmation of what the Lord revealed to me about *my* being responsible to initiate life into my wife's fulfillment.

Something was beginning to happen with me. Signs of life were beginning to appear where a shadow of death lurked for so long.

That week at the School of Pastoral Nurture marked the first full week I had been out of the house since taking ill. Though it was not without difficulty, there came an invasion of hope in knowing that I may be able to resume some degree of a normal life.

As that SPN came to a close, Dick Mills was on hand to speak to us. If you're not familiar with Dick, he most certainly has a prophetic gifting. Here's what he had to say to me:

> "Barry, don't give up on your hopes, your dreams, visions, and aspirations. Know that first God gives the promise, then comes the problem, and finally the performance."

Dick then said the following verses of scripture were what the Lord wanted for me to hold on to:

"For the vision is yet for an appointed time; but at the end it will speak, and it will not lie. Though it tarries, wait for it; because it will surely come. It will not tarry." (Hab 2:3 NKJV)

"Blessed is <u>she</u> who believed, for there will be a fulfillment of those things which were told <u>her</u> from the Lord." (Luke 1:45 NKJV)

"Therefore say to them, 'Thus says the Lord GOD: None of My words will be postponed any more, but the word which I speak will be done,' says the Lord GOD." (Ezek 12:28 NKJV)

"And it will be said in that day: 'Behold, this is our God; We have waited for Him, and He will save us. This is the LORD; We have waited for Him; We will be glad and rejoice in His salvation.'" (Isa 25:9 NKJV)

Then he added, "This is your time, this is it." And this verse is also for you:

"Yet the righteous will hold to his way, and he who has clean hands will be stronger and stronger." (Job 17:9 NKJV)

There was no disclosure to Pastor Jack or to Dick Mills about any of my concerns, disappointments, or apprehensions, or for that matter my medical condition. I had though, prayed with another pastor at the SPN, and asked him to pray that my wife and I would have a child.

Nobody at that SPN class knew how important an issue this was for me, or, for that matter, the struggles I was having with health. Add to that the concerns I had because of the lack of growth in our ministry.

But the fact of the matter is that several prophecies prior to this had come to us in the past, which said that we would have a child and pastor a church. We had God's promise, but could it be that this was now indeed our time?

Nothing short of a miracle was needed for us to have a child.

Nothing short of a miracle was needed for me to regain health.

Nothing short of a miracle was needed for our ministry to grow.

Pastor Jack prayed over each of the pastors in attendance before we left.

Something unusual also happened at this SPN. Traditionally, pastors were required to attend three separate sessions before attending Session IV together with their spouses. While Pastor Jack was sharing with us the benefits of attending together with our spouses, the Lord ministered to him to drop the prerequisites. In so doing, any pastor who attended any one of the sessions could now attend the special Session IV with their spouse.

This opportunity couldn't have come at a better time. Cozzette saw something happening in me as a result of attending the SPN I, and she wanted to be a part of that. So we signed up together for the SPN IV that was coming up in August 2002, about seven months away.

Within a few weeks after that first SPN, Cozzette and I were ready to try again for our child. I can't say the journey was without struggle. In all honesty, it did not appear the most opportune time to pursue having children.

There was my health to consider. I was still lethargic, struggling to breathe, and fighting the pains as well as the overall ill feelings that went along with the pain. My conscious mind was plagued with thoughts of futility. After all, how can life emerge from such a dead situation?

Cozzette was not without her own emotional burdens. In the weeks preceding the medical procedure which was to help us conceive, her father passed away. There were difficult funeral arrangements that had to be made. A dear friend of ours passed away by his own hand the same day as Cozzette's father. A logical mind would have considered this the worst time ever to try to conceive.

But we were not motivated by logic; we were driven by faith, inspired by hope in the promises of God. So we pushed onward in defiance of all appearances of circumstance by faith, striving for the hope of the promise that was well beyond our visible range.

17. Receiving New Life

*Born out of this surrender, Joseph's
middle name was chosen for its spiritual
connotation–obedience*

—ɯ—

In Genesis chapter 20, we see that it was the prayer of a man—Abraham that caused barren wombs to be opened.

In reviewing this it occurred to me that I had never before honestly prayed for Cozzette to bear a child. And so for the first time in our marriage, I cried out through prayer for God to grant us this child.

Within ten days of that prayer, the test results came back— we were pregnant, but we were not out of the woods yet. We were here before. But, this time, we were both praying. The months that followed were wrought with many close calls and difficulties, especially during the first trimester.

Our ministry appeared to be growing ever so slightly. We had an Evangelist join us who served as our Associate Minister. Ben was an answer to prayer. His own past was somewhat speckled with disobedience, as is many of ours. A recent brush with prostate cancer brought him closer to God.

I met Ben one day at the Hometown Buffet in Palmdale. As I approached the table to sit down, there was a tugging in my spirit to speak with him. As we began to talk, it was clear that we were brothers in the Lord. I shared with Ben how Cozzette and I were working to get this fledgling ministry off the ground.

Several weeks latter as we prepared for service, we saw that unique cowboy hat coming towards us. Ben told us that his pastor wanted him to come help is in ministry. What a tremendous blessing!

Without a doubt Ben's joining us marked a turning point in our ministry. He was willing to work as hard as it took to evangelize. Ben and I talked about starting up a Bible study, and soon he was leading our Palmdale Bible study.

Cozzette and I spent a great deal of time with Ben. We sat together talking about the marvels of the Lord often past midnight. Ben loved serving. He sought every opportunity to serve God through our ministry.

Through all of our rushing to the hospital because of the apparent close calls of pregnancy, through all the Sundays that I was just too sick to preach, since his arrival, Ben was there to "hold up" the ministry.

Both of my grandparents passed away during the pregnancy. It seemed as though during that time we were burying a loved one as a matter of routine.

By the August SPN IV, Cozzette and I had just a couple of months remaining in the pregnancy. It was a very serene time, as we received ministering. There was no hiding the fact that Cozzette was pregnant, and we were excited to share with Pastor Jack how the Lord blessed us since the last SPN.

The prophecy and the prayer, it was all coming to pass. Pastor Jack prayed for us and said that with this pregnancy God was birthing "new life" into our ministry as well as our family. For us this was another confirmation. Several weeks earlier, Pastor Robert Colwell of Love and Order Christian Fellowship in Los Angeles told us the exact same thing.

As Dick Mills prophesied earlier that year, this was our time, and we were now beginning to see it coming. What expectation! What joy!

On November 13 2002, at about 10:00 A.M., Joseph Akim was born. Nothing prepared me for the way I would feel when I first saw him. The Doctor had him about half way out and stopped to clean his little nose and mouth. Joseph turned his head and looked at me and gave the biggest smile. It was as if he knew me all the while. My heart melted right there as I gazed into those beautiful little eyes.

His name, Joseph was chosen for its spiritual connotation meaning, "God is adding." It also means, 'Let Him add and keep on adding." Joseph was the long awaited child of Jacob and Rachel, who eventually saved his brothers during the famine.

Akim encompasses the following inherent meanings — to rise, arise, stand, rise up, to stand, to be established, be confirmed, to endure, to be fixed, to be valid, to be proven, to be fulfilled, to persist, to be set, to become powerful, to confirm, to ratify, to carry out, to give effect, to set up, to erect, to build, to constitute, to make binding.

It was clear to me that God was establishing us, in spite of all the illness and difficulties. It was a time when all remnants of self-will and determination yielded beneath the fire of tribulation. It was a time of discovery that came about by virtue of complete surrender in obedience to God. No longer would I seek to do ministry by my own cunning and craftiness. No longer would I seek another vocation.

It was the season of my surrender. No longer would I be able to run from God's calling. No longer would I be able to walk in a pseudo adherence to His will. No longer would I be able to "deal" my way around the road He chose for me.

121

God called me to pastor, not to manage computer networks or engineer aircraft. Not to fulfill my own glory, but to pursue His. Not to draft a ministry from my own skill, but to be completely available to the breath of His leading. I had to "give it all to Him," my life depended on it, my family's life depended on it.

Ministry was not going to be in the image of my computer business. It was not going to be a marriage of my business ideals together with my spiritual understanding. It was not going to be according to my project plans or milestones. It was to be about Jesus, and communicating the life within His Word, lifting up His name.

"And I, if I am lifted up from the earth, will draw all peoples to Myself." (John 12:32 NKJV)

I had come to a place of surrender. A place where my past accomplishments and worldly desires reached an impasse. I was firmly on a new road now, and where I was headed, my pride could no longer follow.

Born out of this surrender, Joseph's middle name was chosen for its spiritual connotation—obedience. He was born at a place where my wrestle with God was concluded. Obedience became the order of the day, for before that I wrestled with God and prevailed. Though I emerged somewhat wounded in my flesh, new life flowed out of a complete dependence on Him.

We had our son.

Our ministry was growing.

18. In Retrospect

And having tasted and found it lacking, He presented me with His call, a road to fullness, a road to destiny.

—ʍ—

After the Lord found me, there were times when I envied those who were brought up in the church. Often I wondered how life would have been different if only I were raised with the Lord. I imagined life would have been richer had I grown up in faith.

Void of the church experience as a youth, I sought vocations that were familiar to me, vocations I identified with through family and environment. My father loved mechanics and exposed me to his passion. He also loved music, and spent much of his leisure time playing the piano and various percussion instruments with his friends. Some of the most joyful memories of my youth were "hanging out" with my dad, either working on cars or playing music with him.

Grandpa was a "sheet metal" engineer and a private pilot. He taught me math and often took me flying with him. He was a quiet man, stern but loving. When we went flying together, there was little conversation. It was just him and I together, soaring through the skies, feeling the wind beneath the airplanes wings.

He would take me through the pre-flight list checking over the airplane. After practicing a few "touch and go" landings, we would fly to a distant airport where we would have lunch together. After a nice quiet lunch overlooking the airport we would fly back. Grandpa loved flying and being around airplanes. I loved being with him.

These were the things that impressed me as a child, and that impression helped forge my career decisions. Not that any of those career choices were invalid, in fact they were each quite respectable in their own right. But they would prove not to be the vocation I was born for.

So why would God choose to use a person such as me in the ministry? Ministry service was something I didn't understand growing up, and at times even loathed. My youth was a life riddled with controversy, problems, and despair. And one thing I knew with certainty was that at least I wasn't ever going to be a preacher.

In the void of my knowledge of Christ, preaching was pure foolishness. As one born "out of season" my younger years were spent contrary to the church of Christ. During my teenage years my friends and I would ridicule church-goers. We viewed them as weak and inconsequential.

In the absence of God, I sought the "street life," finding direction and comfort, for a season, in the company of depravity.

Without Him my life was spinning out of control. Certainly, salvation would have been enough. To rejoice with the Lord of glory, to be made a "new creation," to be transformed into His image, was more than I could ever ask for or think.

But to be called into His service, this was no longer foolishness, but somewhere along the road, it became honor above measure to me.

But why? Why would God even remotely consider using a person such as me for His ministry? And why would He, foreknowing the outcome, why would He open such incredible doors for me in the vocations I once sought?

It can be argued that since God opens doors that no man can open, and closes doors that no man could close, that I missed a world of opportunities with respect to my career. Certainly, had I decided to stay with Lockheed I would have remained in the engineering field in a highly coveted and respectable job. Likewise, had I remained in the computer field my family and I would have enjoyed a comfortable living.

So why would God open such bountiful a career path, if in fact an alternate path was His plan for me all along? It's certainly not the way I would design an apprenticeship.

The answer to these questions can be found in the scriptures.

"And we know that all things work together for good to those who love God, to those who are the called according to His purpose. For whom He foreknew, He also predestined to be conformed to the image of His Son, that He might be the firstborn among many brethren. Moreover whom He predestined, these He also called; whom He called, these He also justified; and whom He justified, these He also glorified." (Rom 8:28-30 NKJV)

All things, even the malignity of my broken past, its successes, its failures, the hurts as well as the healing, all things work together for good by virtue of a heart turned towards God, and the calling He places upon that heart.

And in His foreknowledge, He predestined a transformation, He detailed a plan and a purpose, and He gave a calling.

125

And because of His intended purpose, His calling, God alone justifies us, in spite of the snares of our past.

And He, as a loving father, accomplishes this with His kind intention towards us.

Because He did not say to me in the beginning, "This is My chosen career for you, follow it or else. . ." But with a strong arm and a loving hand He allowed me to see the fullness of the road to my own vanities, by allowing me to taste of the world's glory, which glory is passing away.

And having tasted and found it lacking, He presented me with His call, a road to fullness, a road to destiny. Having knowledge of the first, the choice is now mine. If He would have presented the better choice first I would have always wondered if I made the right decision. My heart would have been divided between His mission, and my longing to know what life could have been.

But now God is glorified, in that the one who has "tasted" of the richness of the former career has found it to be insignificant when compared to the greatness of His calling.

By "opening doors" into other careers, God has given me a choice. And through this choice it has become settled in my spirit, that for Christ I live, and His call is my only desire.

And because it is not the career that I sought after but one that was given to me by God, my flesh can never take credit for it. I can never glory as though my cleverness has earned any accomplishment, but all I have and all I have to give are His.

Truly God does use the weak things as the scripture says:

> *"For you see your calling, brethren, that not many wise according to the flesh, not many mighty, not many noble, are called. But God has chosen the foolish things of the world to put to shame the wise, and God has chosen the weak things of the world to*

126

put to shame the things which are mighty; and the base things of the world and the things which are despised God has chosen, and the things which are not, to bring to nothing the things that are, that no flesh should glory in His presence." (1 Cor 1:26-29 NKJV)

I have in this found a law, that the glory of my flesh is enmity with God, but my soul rejoices in the glory He bestows upon me.

19. On the Road to Glory

—ɷ—

Many of us as children first pursue glory on the merry-go-round. It was that shiny brass ring held slightly out of reach. As we got older various allures of life replaced the brass ring.

There are many things that hold luster in an appearance of glory.

"There is one glory of the sun, another glory of the moon, and another glory of the stars; for one star differs from another star in glory." (1 Cor 15:41 NKJV)

If we are not careful, the things we esteem glorious, the things we reach for and, in fact, obtain will eventually lose their luster—just as does the brass ring.

As I glance back over all the career choices and opportunities that presented themselves in my life, one thing becomes clear. Success in job fulfillment, success in entrepreneurship, success in any vocation is meaningless apart from a successful relationship with Christ.

It's all empty ambition and fruitless futility, to try to attain fulfillment apart from Him.

There are many pursuits we can embark upon, many pathways whose signposts provide an allure of fulfillment. But the world cannot hold true to its promises. And its glitter will all give place to dust.

There is only one true glory that is good, that is the glory of God. It is the glory of His presence, as He gives Himself to those who are His. Nothing else can last. Nothing else can fulfill. And this is the glory that will never fade.

To find it takes a heart of surrender, a heart willing to release preconceived notions and fruitless vanity. It takes a softened knee before Him in prayer, "Lord God of all, show me your way." It takes knowing, surrendering, and yielding to His voice.

Vocation is not the issue. What is at issue is to live with a certainty that whatever it is that we do, our walk is in pursuit of closeness with Him. That whatever career path we choose, it is the one He chose for us, and at the end of that road we rest assured that God awaits us with open arms saying, *"Well done, good and faithful servant."*

The road to glory only comes as we make our way to Him. It may not be the most glamorous road. It may not even be popular. It's not preoccupied with fancy cars, seeks no self aggrandizement, and it's often the road less traveled.

In Matthew chapter seven, Jesus declares:

"Enter by the narrow gate; for wide is the gate and broad is the way that leads to destruction, and there are many who go in by it. Because narrow is the gate and difficult is the way which leads to life, and there are few who find it." (Mat 7:13-14 NKJV)

We all choose the roads we take. In our choices we can forge a way into our own will, or we can be sensitive to His leading.

My own life has been rich with opportunities beyond my wildest imagination. Yet, as I continue down the road, the allure and distractions fade, giving way to an incredible light. In the brilliance of that light the journey is made clear.

All the pathways I chose in pursuit of personal glory, all the careers I once held dear—Performing Arts, Aircraft Engineering, Entrepreneurship, and Computer Network Management—I view them all and count them as loss.

As I reflect on so bountiful a career, there is only one career choice that becomes acceptable. There is a song that so beautifully captures my heart on this issue:

> All I once held dear, built my life upon,
> All this world reveres and wars to own;
> All I once thought gain, I have counted loss,
> Spent and worthless now compared to this.

> Knowing You, Jesus, knowing You
> There is no greater thing.
> You're my all, You're the best,
> You're my joy, my righteousness,
> And I love You, Lord.

> Now my heart's desire is to know You more,
> To be found in You and known as Yours,
> To possess by faith what I could not earn,
> All surpassing gift of righteousness

> Oh, to know the power of Your risen life,
> And to know You in Your sufferings;
> To become like You in Your death, my Lord,
> So with You to live and never die.

Knowing You, Jesus, knowing You
There is no greater thing.
You're my all, You're the best,
You're my joy, my righteousness,
And I love You Lord.

©1993 Make Way Music
Words and Music by Graham Kendrick

For all of the performances I played, all of the blueprints
I've laid, the computers I've made, these were merely rest
stops, slight detours if you will, on the road to glory.

Printed in the United States
202551BV00001B/106-168/P

9 781604 774603